BEFORE "I DO"

THE LAWYER'S GUIDE TO PROPOSING A PRENUP

LESLIE L. ABRIGO, ESQ.

Difference Press

Washington DC, USA

Copyright © Leslie L. Abrigo, 2024

All rights reserved. No part of this book may be reproduced in any form without permission in writing from the author. Reviewers may quote brief passages in reviews.

Published 2024

Disclaimer: Leslie L. Abrigo is a lawyer licensed to practice law in California, only. Nothing in this book is intended to serve as legal advice. The information provided in this book should not be used as a substitute for obtaining legal advice. You should always consult a suitably qualified attorney regarding any specific legal problem or matter in your local area. Use of this book does not create an attorney-client relationship between the reader, Leslie L Abrigo, or her law firm. This book is for general information only.

No part of this publication may be reproduced or transmitted in any form or by any means, mechanical or electronic, including photocopying or recording, or by any information storage and retrieval system, or transmitted by email without permission in writing from the author.

Neither the author nor the publisher assumes any responsibility for errors, omissions, or contrary interpretations of the subject matter herein. Any perceived slight of any individual or organization is purely unintentional.

Brand and product names are trademarks or registered trademarks of their respective owners.

Cover design: Jennifer Stimson

Editing: Madeline Kosten

For Ruby, Conan, and my mom, Tina. We did it!

CONTENTS

1. I Work Hard for My Money — 1
2. Finding the Right Lawyer — 9
3. What You Need to Know — 17
4. A Prenup Is Not Something One Does on a Whim — 25
5. The Terms of the Prenup — 33
6. What Happens When You Do Not Get a Prenup in California — 43
7. Protecting the Money Given to You — 53
8. The House You Bought Before Marriage — 63
9. Reimbursements for Stuff Paid for before Marriage — 71
10. Protecting Your Income and Retirement — 79
11. A Gift May Not Always Be a Gift — 91
12. Staying out of Your Fiancé's Potential Legal Issues — 99
13. Children and Child Support — 109
14. Spousal Support — 119
15. How to Break the News That You Want a Prenup — 129
16. Roadblocks to a Prenup — 137
17. There Go the Wedding Bells — 145

Acknowledgments — 155
About the Author — 157
About Difference Press — 159
Other Books by Difference Press — 163
Gift for Reader — 165

1

I WORK HARD FOR MY MONEY

You've built a life you're proud of, a life that reflects years of hard work, dedication, and personal sacrifice. You were able to get through your undergraduate and graduate studies without having to take on any student loan debt. After your formal education, you were able to climb the corporate ladder. Your hard work allowed you to make shrewd investment decisions. Every step was meticulously planned.

A year ago, you met your fiancé, who has her own career and business. After several months of dating, she moved into your house from her tiny condo. You even got a dog. You are financially responsible for most of your shared living expenses because you earn significantly more than she does. While she contributes to shared living expenses, such as utilities and groceries, there is no way that she could have ever qualified on her own for the mortgage you got for the home you bought before your relationship. You not only had a significant down payment through savings, but your income was also enough to qualify for a home in a neighborhood known for homes that are currently worth upwards of $2 million.

You have met each other's parents, and things are falling into place quickly and easily. She is definitely the one. You have asked her to marry you. But now, as you stand on the brink of a new chapter with the person you love, there's an important conversation you've been avoiding: the prenuptial agreement.

You have been thinking of a prenuptial agreement for a while. Your parents have significant investments that you will most likely inherit. You even help them manage their real estate investments from time to time. Now that they are retired and getting older, the concerns about what you are going to be doing in terms of starting a family have been the topic of many embarrassing family conversations.

Since they have been planning their futures, they have also brought up the topic of a prenuptial agreement. It is not like they do not like your fiancé. But you and your parents are aware of several divorces involving friends and family that were horrific in terms of emotional and mental suffering as well as significant financial costs. They don't want their hard-earned assets going to anyone other than you and their, yet to be born, grandchildren. Moreover, they don't want any gifts that they give to you to get tied up in a divorce or used to pay for a divorce in the event that you need to ask them for funds to pay attorney fees. Your parents have been together for your entire life, and while they believe in love, they also know that marriage is hard, and they have worked their entire lives so that you were able to get where you are in life. They want to create a financial legacy and that could be derailed by a divorce in the family.

But for months, you've been caught up in the whirlwind of wedding preparations. You proposed with a stunning Tiffany ring, which she chose. You planned an unforgettable engagement, and both of you have spent countless hours and financial resources ensuring every detail of the wedding is perfect. Something, however, is gnawing at the back of your mind. Your fiancé, the love of your life, has been living in the home you purchased before you met her, a house you've diligently paid off month by month. She now refers to the house as "our" house, and while you intend to live in it after marriage, it makes you uneasy.

Throughout the relationship, you've shouldered most of the financial responsibilities because your income significantly outpaces hers. It is not as if she doesn't have her own money. She contributes to the shared living expenses by paying for other things. It's a dynamic that has worked well until now, but as the wedding day approaches, you have been withdrawn, and it seems as if there's an undeniable tension in the air.

You've always known that protecting your assets was important. While your parents have been gentle but persistent, they have increased their reminders of the importance of a prenup. Yet, despite their advice, you've postponed this conversation, perhaps for fear of rocking the boat or appearing mistrustful.

Now, with only a month left before the wedding and relatives already booking their flights, the pressure is on. You can no longer afford to put off the discussion. You are fully aware that the more time that goes by, the more that this discussion could derail the entire wedding. You do not want this to blindside her.

So, to keep you from getting in this position, this

chapter is here to help you understand why a prenuptial agreement is not just a safeguard for you, but is also a protection for both of you, ensuring clarity and fairness as you embark on your married life together. Just having a discussion about a prenuptial agreement can provide you both with clarity about life goals and long-term financial planning. It is an absolute necessity to have these kinds of conversations before getting married because, once you are married, you do not want to have any surprises that would sour the relationship.

UNDERSTANDING THE NECESSITY OF A PRENUP

The first step in navigating this delicate conversation is understanding why a prenuptial agreement is essential. It's not just about protecting your current assets; it's about planning for a future that's built on transparency and mutual respect. Here are some critical reasons why you need a prenup.

Protection of Premarital Assets

The house you live in, the one you bought with your hard-earned money, is a significant investment. Moreover, since working your way up the corporate ladder, you have acquired significant deferred compensation and retirement accounts. Community property is the legal term used to define any property or debts acquired from the date of marriage to the date of separation. In the event of divorce, a state that has adopted a community property rule for acquisition of martial property, will divide those assets and debts equally between the parties. That means all property and debts acquired from the date of marriage to the date of separation and any accrued interest is divided 50-50. In a community property state like California, without a prenup, the assets you acquired before marriage could acquire a community property interest, in which your spouse would have a right to an interest. Perhaps you would not mind sharing your assets with your fiancé after several years of marriage, but without a prenup, you do not get that choice. Furthermore, the status of using the term "ours" could create contentious issues in the event of a divorce causing increased attorney fees and costs. A prenup can clearly delineate what assets remain separate property.

Clarifying Financial Expectations

A prenuptial agreement can help set clear financial boundaries and expectations. While you have a job and upward mobility in that job, your fiancé does not have that. She has her own business and is self-employed. You have not really discussed with her what her business debts and obligations might be. You also know that she is still paying off her student loans. Perhaps she has big plans that might involve significant financial risk, or perhaps she may not want to share with you any increase in the value of her business or business income. Clarity in the form of a written agreement can prevent misunderstandings and conflicts over money in the future, contributing to a healthier and more transparent relationship.

Safeguarding Future Inheritance

As you are expecting to receive an inheritance, a prenup can ensure it remains yours, protected from potential claims in a divorce. This is particularly important if your family has worked hard to build a legacy that they intend to pass down through generations. During the marriage, they may want to give you gifts, only you, or make gifts to both of you. Her parents may also feel the same way and may want to leave an inheritance for her. Thus, it is important to plan in advance, what you might do with that money or property and how those might be used during marriage. Moreover, if those assets generate any income, you will want to clearly define what the character of that income would be along with how you characterize any work efforts you put into management of those assets.

Debt Protection

Not all financial concerns are about assets. If either of you brings debt into the marriage, a prenup can help ensure that you aren't held responsible for your partner's premarital liabilities, protecting your financial future. It could also shield you from liability caused by business-related lawsuits.

Future Career and Income Considerations

You could completely opt out of a community property marriage. Your career trajectory and earning potential are part of the financial picture. Changing positions or jobs will affect your standard of living, and with the passage of time, investment accounts could be rolled over into other accounts or acquired by a different investment company making them hard to trace in the event of a long-term marriage at the time of divorce.

You may want to have children. You should be clear as to expectations about continuing in a career that might take either of you away from the children for a significant period of time as that means that one of you will need to be the primary caregiver of the children and could put a big pause on their career or stifle future income. Thus, a discussion about spousal support should be had. A prenup can address how these factors are managed in the marriage, particularly as there is already a significant income disparity between you and your fiancé.

By addressing the topic of a prenuptial agreement with sensitivity and respect, you can turn a potentially difficult conversation into an opportunity for greater understanding and cooperation. This chapter has laid the foundation for understanding why a prenup is necessary, not just for you but for the health of your marriage. In the next chapters, we'll delve deeper into the specifics of drafting an agreement that reflects both of your needs and aspirations, ensuring that your journey into married life is built on a solid, mutually agreed upon foundation.

2

FINDING THE RIGHT LAWYER

Finding the right lawyer to draft your prenuptial agreement is one of the most critical steps in protecting your future. This chapter aims to help you understand the importance of choosing an experienced and trustworthy attorney, someone who can guide you through the process with expertise and sensitivity. Allow me to share why my experience as a divorce attorney for over twenty years makes me well-equipped to provide the advice and guidance you need.

Choosing a lawyer with extensive experience in family law is paramount. Most people will choose a lawyer in the state in which they plan to live after marriage. As a State Bar of California-certified family law attorney, I have spent more than two decades navigating the complexities of divorce and prenuptial agreements. My interest in this area of practice continues to be in the various legal issues that come up in what some would call a run-of-the-mill case. The practice requires most well-established family law attorneys to have some experience in a wide variety of matters, such as business formation, trusts and estates, and retirement planning. The range of topics in this area of law always makes my days interesting and it's what has kept me interested this long. My experience has shown me the importance of crafting agreements that are clear, fair, and legally sound.

In the process of drafting and negotiating the terms of a prenuptial agreement, I have seen the difference between couples who discuss their terms in advance of meeting with me and those who had no idea what their fiancé wanted and planned. I have been the first one, in some cases, to break the news of not only their fiancé's desire to obtain a prenuptial agreement, but then to also explain the terms of the contract. It is often a horrible conversation with many tears shed. I can only imagine the conversation between the couple when a party leaves my office.

As you are taking steps to prevent hurt feelings and to deepen your understanding between you and your partner, this will make the process less traumatic and go smoothly. Once you get to the point where you are considering a lawyer from a small pool of lawyers, you should already know whether your fiancé is going to sign a prenuptial agreement and what the basic terms of that agreement will be. Your attorney will probably ask more questions of you in order to make sure your agreement covers the most likely future scenarios possible, but if it requires any further discussion with your fiancé, everything will be above board and no surprises will come up.

I understand that you might feel overwhelmed by this process. Many couples are deeply in love and focused on the romance and excitement of planning a wedding. The idea of discussing a prenuptial agreement might seem unromantic or even cynical. However, it's essential to recognize that a thoroughly discussed intention to obtain a well-drafted prenuptial agreement can strengthen your relationship by fostering open and honest communication about financial matters.

Choosing the right lawyer can feel like a daunting task, especially when you're already juggling the many demands of wedding planning. Therefore, it is not recommended that you wait until the last minute to start looking for an attorney. Here are some key factors to consider when selecting an attorney to draft your prenuptial agreement.

SPECIALIZATION IN FAMILY LAW

Ensure that the lawyer specializes in family law and has significant experience with prenuptial agreements. You would be surprised how many family law attorneys do not draft prenuptial agreements. You would also be surprised at how many lawyers, who are not family law specialists, draft an unenforceable prenuptial agreement. Specialization in the state of California not only means they have taken a test that is administered by the Board of Legal Specialization of the State Bar of California, but they are also up-to-date with the latest legal standards and can offer nuanced advice tailored to your situation.

REPUTATION AND REVIEWS

Look for a lawyer with a strong reputation in the field. This can be demonstrated not just by word-of-mouth referrals to this attorney but through peer-acknowledgement, such as awards. While it is important to check reviews and testimonials from previous clients, relying solely on Google may give you skewed results. Keep in mind that many opposing parties in a divorce or disgruntled parents in the event of attorneys who represent children take to the internet to bash attorneys. Thus, personal referrals from friends or family members who have gone through a similar process can also be invaluable. If your friends and family recommend the same attorneys, then you know who you should call.

COMMUNICATION SKILLS

Your lawyer should be an excellent communicator, capable of explaining complex legal concepts in a way that you can understand so that you are able to then have a conversation with your fiancé about any concerns raised by your lawyer. They should be patient and willing to answer all your questions, no matter how trivial they may seem. In this day and age, you may find that lawyers are very keen to respond to or communicate with you via email. This is a preferred method of communication because it tracks communication between you and your lawyer, and it makes clear what advice was provided to you. Should you have any questions, you can go back to that written communication, or you can send another email. But in addition to the emails, your lawyer will meet with you in person or by video conference. If you find it difficult to get your attorney on the phone, schedule an appointment to meet. Like you, your attorney is likely just as busy, but they should not be so busy that they cannot meet with you via appointment.

EMPATHY AND UNDERSTANDING

Since prenuptial agreements can be an emotional topic, it's crucial to find a lawyer who is empathetic and understands the emotional aspects of this process. They should be able to handle sensitive discussions with care and professionalism and likewise give you suggestions for how to approach a sensitive topic with your fiancé and provide you with several options to form the basis of your discussion. Not only will this demonstrate the level of your attorney's care on the task of helping you complete your prenuptial agreement, but it will also demonstrate experience both practically and emotionally.

TRANSPARENT FEES

Discuss the lawyer's fees upfront, both with your fiancé and lawyer. A good lawyer will provide a clear breakdown of their costs and ensure there are no hidden charges. Moreover, your lawyer should provide you with a contract called a retainer agreement. This agreement is required by every lawyer before they begin work. It will contain all of the terms of service and costs associated with service. It is important to read the retainer agreement and ask questions. A lawyer will answer your questions about the contract. This transparency is essential to avoid any surprises down the road.

You may be responsible for the payment of attorney fees for your fiancé. In most of the cases where I represented the party who was initiating the preparation and drafting of the agreement, the other party was usually not in the same income bracket. With a requirement in California that both parties have legal representation and legal advice as to rights that are being waived in a prenuptial agreement, it may behoove you to pay for the attorney's fees for your fiancé to make sure that this requirement is met. It is to your benefit to follow the law with regard to prenuptial agreements to make sure that in the event of divorce, the agreement is enforceable.

MY APPROACH AS A FAMILY LAW ATTORNEY

Over the years, I have worked with many clients who were interested in a prenuptial agreement but did not understand the importance of bringing the topic up with their fiancé. In California, the process of obtaining a signed prenuptial agreement must be completely above board. This means that a written agreement is exchanged between the parties with time for comment and negotiation. It is something where by law, both parties must be represented by legal counsel or receive the equivalent in legal advice. Therefore, I believe in being completely upfront about the process and encourage my clients to talk to their fiancé about terms long before I start drafting an agreement.

Clients can sometimes feel that bringing up the topic might jeopardize their relationship. You should think about why you have this fear. If your fiancé does not want to sign a prenuptial agreement, you must know why. If you and your fiancé have a shared understanding of the purpose of the agreement and work on the agreement's terms cooperatively, you know that your marriage will start off on the right foot. It may be worth it just to ask early on in your relationship if your boyfriend/girlfriend will sign a prenuptial agreement just to make sure you don't waste time on a person who is not on the same page.

It may be better to end it before marriage and suffering through arguments or a costly divorce. In sum, my approach is to help couples see a prenup not as a sign of mistrust, but as a practical step toward ensuring a fair and secure future for both parties. If you cannot even have this conversation with your fiancé, it should be considered a red flag.

Here's how I can help you navigate this process.

Personalized Consultation

I start with a personalized consultation to understand your specific needs and concerns. This initial meeting allows me to tailor my advice to your unique situation and address any immediate questions you might have. For those who may not be aware, I have created a separate workbook that complements this book. If you have not already purchased the workbook, before our first consultation, I will provide you with a copy of *The Prenup Workbook: A Different Kind of Marriage Planning*. You and your fiancé will then be given time to fill it out and gather the documents referenced in the workbook.

Clear and Fair Agreements

Once you have completed the workbook and provided the required documents, I will draft the agreement and meet with you to go over a draft to discuss if it meets your ideal terms. My goal is to draft an agreement that is clear, fair, and legally binding. I take the time to explain each clause and its implications, ensuring that both you and your fiancé are comfortable with the terms. Once the agreement is to your satisfaction, we will send it off to your fiancé's attorney, and a copy of the agreement will be given to you to provide to your fiancé.

Balancing Emotions and Practicality

I recognize that emotions run high when discussing finances and future planning. I strive to balance these emotions with practical advice, helping you both see the benefits of having a well-drafted prenup. I will make myself available to answer your questions.

Ongoing Support

Even after the prenup is signed, I remain available to provide ongoing support and answer any questions that may arise. My commitment is to ensure that you feel confident and secure in your decision and how to handle issues going forward.

Moving Forward

Remember, a prenuptial agreement is not just a legal document; it's a step toward mutual respect and understanding. By choosing the right lawyer and approaching this process thoughtfully, you can protect your assets while also honoring your relationship. Let's move forward with confidence and clarity.

3

WHAT YOU NEED TO KNOW

Now that we've established the importance of a prenuptial agreement and how to find the right lawyer to help you draft one, it's time to look at the bigger picture. This chapter will provide a roadmap of the topics we'll cover in this book, giving you a clear understanding of what to expect and how a prenuptial agreement can address various issues. By the end of this process, you will have an agreement that both you and your partner can live with, one that fosters transparency and mutual respect.

SETTING THE STAGE

Before diving into the specifics, it's essential to grasp the overarching purpose and scope of prenuptial agreements. Chapters 4 through 16 delve into various aspects and considerations that should go into planning for a prenuptial agreement, including legal steps, asset protection, debt protection, spousal support, and things that a prenuptial agreement cannot protect. Learning about all of these issues will help in shaping your understanding of prenups' multifaceted nature.

A WELL THOUGHT-OUT PLAN

In Chapter 4, we discuss the importance of the timelines for careful planning that will not result in additional stress right before the wedding. Not only might there be statutory timelines in your state as to when parties might be able to sign the prenuptial agreement, but if the topic was never discussed prior to engagement, it could lead to heated discussions and potentially postponing or canceling the wedding. It is best to be prepared by having the conversation early on in the relationship.

THE TERMS OF THE PRENUP

Chapter 5 emphasizes the importance of open communication and collaboration in broaching the topic of prenups with your partner. By fostering trust and empathy, you can create a supportive environment for discussing sensitive financial matters and reaching a mutually beneficial agreement.

It will also discuss the kinds of topics that might be protected by the prenup.

- **Asset Protection**: Defining which assets are considered individual property and which are marital property.
- **Debt Responsibility**: Clarifying responsibility for any premarital and marital debts.

- **Income, Investments and Retirement Plans:** Outlining how income and investments will be handled during the marriage along with beneficiary designations and survivor benefits.
- **Inheritance and Other Gifts:** Ensuring that future inheritances, gifts from family, and gifts between spouses remain separate property.
- **Spousal Support:** Discussing potential spousal support arrangements in the event of a divorce.

By understanding these components, you and your partner can work together to create an agreement that addresses your specific needs and concerns.

NAVIGATING THE PROCESS

Chapter 6 outlines the practical steps involved in the prenup process, from initiating negotiations to finalizing the agreement. Specifically, we will explore the California community property standard upon divorce regarding management of assets and debts in marriages that do not have prenuptial agreements. We will also talk about practical problems that come when managing assets, debts, and gifts without a prenuptial agreement during marriage.

In addition, you will learn:

- How your separate property house could acquire a community property interest during marriage.

- How liabilities are created between unmarried persons.
- How your interest in deferred compensation or other ownership interests in your company/employer may acquire a community property interest.
- How income acquired during marriage could be community property.
- How gifts between spouses before marriage and gifts during marriage are treated upon divorce.
- How risky business interests and marital debt are divided by the court upon divorce in community property states like California.
- How the court handles child custody and support in the event of divorce.
- How spousal support is determined in California in the event of divorce.

GETTING INTO THE NITTY GRITTY

In Chapter 7, we will talk about protecting money from your parents. In this chapter, we will dive into gifts from family by putting them into two categories: gifts from family while they are alive and gifts from family via inheritance. You will learn how gifts can be misconstrued as gifts to both parties during marriage. We will discuss how commingling separate and community property will make things tricky in the event of divorce. We will brush upon reimbursement rights between spouses for separate property used to obtain or pay down community property. Finally, we will discuss how family pressure might affect the way in which you term items in your prenuptial agreement.

In Chapter 8, we will talk about the house you bought before marriage. You will learn about how living in a separate property home with your fiancé before marriage could affect a divorce. We will discuss mortgage payments and mortgages including the treatment of refinances of real estate (or what is referred to as real property among attorneys) during marriage if there is no prenuptial agreement. We will also get into rental property income, how that is treated in the event of divorce if there is no prenup.

Chapter 9 delves into reimbursements for things that you may have paid for before marriage either for your fiancé or for the both of you. We will talk about the liabilities you may have accumulated with your fiancé prior to marriage to include the costs and potential debt you may hold as a result of an expensive reception and wedding as well as the rings.

Chapter 10 is about protecting your income and your retirement. This chapter explores strategies for safeguarding your income, retirement, and business interests during marriage both with and without a prenuptial agreement. We will look at bonuses, employer-sponsored retirement contributions, stock, stock options and stock agreements, and work efforts. We will also look at possible ways to protect business partners.

In Chapter 11, we get into what qualifies as a gift. We talk about how gifts during marriage may not actually be found by a court to be a gift upon divorce. We will discuss how the importance of the marital standard of living may affect the value of gifts made during divorce, in the absence of a prenuptial agreement. We will also look into how you can clearly define a gift made during marriage in your prenuptial agreement by defining the value of those gifts and or creating a separate writing of the intent to gift property to your fiancé.

Chapter 12 discussed staying out of your fiancé's potential legal issues. This chapter addresses the assumption of business risk and legal problems during marriage, absent a prenuptial agreement. We will talk about shielding your fiancé from potentially high-risk business dealings during marriage with the use of a prenuptial agreement. We get into how you cannot use prenuptial agreements to shield your fiancé from their own creditors, but we can limit your fiancé's exposure to your creditors' claims and vice versa via satisfaction of debt/judgments by limiting community property characterization of debt.

Chapter 13 explores the possibility of children and child support. We will talk about public policy in California regarding children and child support and how child support is typically calculated in the event of a divorce. We will get into artificial reproductive technology and embryo assignments as a potential topic of concern in a prenuptial agreement.

Chapter 14 delves into one of the most sought-after terms to be included in a prenuptial agreement, and that is the issue of spousal support. We will discuss spousal support laws in California including martial standard of living and income of the parties at the time of divorce. We will discuss limitations to spousal support terms in prenuptial agreements, and we will discuss potential obstacles to an agreement in support of no spousal support where a large income disparity between the parties may trigger legal complexities in the event of divorce.

BREAKING THE NEWS

Chapter 15 will discuss how to break the news to your fiancé that you want a prenuptial agreement. This chapter provides invaluable tips for initiating a conversation about prenups with your partner, emphasizing the importance of honesty, empathy, and active listening in fostering open communication and mutual understanding. We will discuss the importance of the timing of a discussion that would include your desire to obtain a prenuptial agreement as well as the timing you should include in getting an agreement prepared with mutually agreeable terms.

ROADBLOCKS TO A PRENUP

Chapter 16 discusses roadblocks in obtaining a prenuptial agreement. This chapter explores the potential obstacles and challenges you may encounter in the prenup process, from financial considerations to emotional concerns. We will discuss strategies for overcoming these roadblocks and achieving a successful outcome with an agreement that is satisfactory to both of you. We will further discuss what happens when a spouse attempts to set aside a prenuptial agreement while going through divorce. We will talk about terms in a prenuptial agreement that may not be enforceable and what the court does with agreements that are partially unenforceable.

Chapter 17 will be a summary of all the things you learned in this book. As we conclude our exploration of prenuptial agreements, you'll be equipped with a comprehensive overview of the prenup journey. By embracing open communication, commencing in a timely manner, and understanding that negotiation is an important process that will create mutual understanding of the life goals that each of you has, you'll be well-prepared to navigate the legal process to obtain a mutually satisfactory prenuptial agreement with confidence and clarity, laying the groundwork for a secure and prosperous marital journey.

4

A PRENUP IS NOT SOMETHING ONE DOES ON A WHIM

A prenuptial agreement is a significant legal document that requires careful planning, discussion, and execution. It's not something that can be hastily put together at the last minute before your wedding. In this chapter, we'll explore the legal steps involved in creating a prenuptial agreement and provide you with a timeline to help you navigate this process smoothly.

THE IMPORTANCE OF PLANNING AHEAD

Crafting a prenuptial agreement takes time. It's not just about the legal drafting; it's about having meaningful conversations with your fiancé and ensuring that both parties fully understand and agree to the terms. This process can take several months, and attempting to rush it just before the wedding can lead to unnecessary stress and potential legal complications.

STEP-BY-STEP

To help you understand the timeline and the necessary steps, I will break down the prenuptial agreement process so that you can understand not only why it is important to plan ahead, but also to encourage open conversation about your life goals early on in your relationship.

Pursuant to the current laws in the state of California (2024), there must be a minimum of seven days between when a person is presented with a final version of a prenuptial agreement and when they sign it. There are also a number of other requirements including that each has what basically amounts to legal representation. This assumes that you don't want the agreement thrown out and set aside by the court in litigation during a potential divorce matter. Therefore, knowing that there is a waiting period before one can sign an agreement, this is not something to put off until right before your wedding day. Moreover, you don't want to derail the wedding process while throwing a potential negotiation in the mix while you are tasting wedding cakes. So, having solidified the basic terms with your fiancé prior to the enlistment of an attorney to draft your prenuptial agreement would make the entire process run smoother.

If you are serious about finding your potential spouse while dating, then you may have already asked key questions about life goals. Understandably, not everyone starts a relationship with a person with the intention of making that person their spouse. As a divorce attorney with over twenty years of experience, I have seen people get together for all kinds of reasons, and I can sincerely tell you that some of these people were not thinking about finances when they got married.

So even though I think this is needless to say, it should not be taken for granted that you and your fiancé are on the same page in terms of protecting your financial future, even if you think you have had the I-want-a-prenup conversation. Communication is subjective and people have different communication styles. Effective communication requires understanding and respecting these differences. Therefore, it is crucial to engage in clear, honest, and open communication with your fiancé. As a visual learner, things do not make complete sense to me unless I can read it. You might be the same as me. Therefore, having had a conversation about what you want may not have registered with your fiancé, and vice versa.

A judge once told me that he is often surprised about the way in which parties express the same series of events. He explained that while they testified under oath that they were at the same event at the same time, each version of events was conveyed as if they were not even at the same place together, and each person believed what they were saying was the truth.

So, you will want to start a series of conversations about what each of you wants to get out of a prenuptial agreement. You will want to do this several months before your wedding so that you can address mutual concerns in a thoughtful way. In this way, a few things could happen:

1. You have an agreement regarding basic terms that each of you would agree to and that would lead you into the next phase of prenuptial preparation.
2. You realize that you are not on the same page, and may need more time before you get married, by enlisting the help of a relationship

counselor or attorney to help guide your conversations so that you eventually work out the basic terms of an agreement that you could both live with.
3. You realize that your fiancé is not the person for you. Regardless of what happens, either scenario should lead to you getting what you want, and most importantly, it should prevent an expensive and potentially financially disastrous divorce.

My workbook, *The Prenup Workbook: A Different Kind of Marriage Planning*, will assist you in this discussion. The purpose of the workbook is to help you and your fiancé get organized regarding preparation of terms, timelines, and documents you will need when you meet with your lawyers. It also helps ask pivotal questions to one another to literally get on the same page with what your prenuptial agreement will say.

Once you and your fiancé have a basic idea of what terms will go into the prenup, you should decide who you will be hiring. Contrary to some beliefs, in California, it is highly recommended that each party is represented by counsel to draft and explain their rights prior to signing the agreement. I have seen prenuptial agreements drafted by persons who were both unrepresented, and those agreements were set aside, not just for the fact that neither had counsel, but because the terms were unconscionable. So, it's best to let the lawyers do the lawyering and drafting of binding legal contracts.

Again, each of you will want to have your own attorneys. Sometimes, one person will hire one attorney first to draft the agreement, and then once a draft is complete, the second lawyer is hired to represent the other party to review the agreement and potentially negotiate different terms. Either way, one of the attorneys has to draft the agreement, and if you are the one asking for a prenuptial agreement, it should be your lawyer who drafts it. Primarily because they will put in all the terms that you want and agreed to with your fiancé, and it will most likely cost more to hire that lawyer since more of their time will be devoted to preparing the agreement than the other attorney.

You will also want to hire attorneys who are state-certified family law specialists. In California, the Board of Legal Specialization for the State Bar of California administers a test to attorneys to allow them to represent themselves as specialists. These attorneys, for the most part, have a higher-level understanding of family law. You do not want to retain an attorney who solely drafts contracts or solely drafts wills and trusts, because while they are also lawyers and they have experience drafting contracts, I have seen too many big mistakes that were made in the execution of the agreements that lead to attorney malpractice claims because the agreements were unenforceable.

Additionally, there is a certain level of financial disclosure that must be made prior to the signing of the prenuptial agreement. Attorneys who are family law specialists should know the amount of disclosure that must be made to create an agreement that is based on sufficient knowledge that would allow your fiancé to sign off, fully aware of what she was getting into. Part of this financial disclosure will include freely divulging income, assets, and debts. I have seen this done in a number of ways, but the bottom line is that your fiancé needs to have enough information to make an informed decision. Each attorney usually completes this part of the process for their own client. Depending on the size and complexity of your estate, assets, and debts, this could be a time-consuming process as your attorney could require you to provide financial records in support of the terms stated in your prenuptial agreement.

After hiring your attorney and providing them with sufficient financial information to get started, your attorney will draft the agreement after you have had discussions about the terms of the agreement. Once a draft is completed, you will again discuss the agreement and its terms until it is to a point where you feel comfortable providing your agreement to your fiancé and / or her attorney. I will usually have a few drafts that get passed between me and my client to make sure that the terms of the agreement are to their satisfaction. I often have Spanish-speaking clients as I am bilingual and sometimes that will require translations either of documents that I am provided by my client, or a translation needs to be made of the agreement itself. So, it is important that whoever you hire has enough time to obtain whatever tools/services are necessary to make sure the agreement is understandable to you and your fiancé.

Once the agreement is provided to your fiancé and / or her attorney, it is time for her attorney to explain the legal significance of the terms to her. Do not be surprised if your fiancé wants to edit the agreement or negotiate terms. Most people are not aware of the legal waivers that are a part of a prenuptial agreement, and thus for the first time are being informed about them by their lawyer. So, while you both planned to do certain things prior to retaining lawyers, it is normal to modify terms that may not be what was initially planned. This is why both of you have lawyers, and your lawyers will help you insert terms that reflect the intentions that both of you had prior to retaining lawyers. That said, evidence that there was a negotiation process and that terms were modified to your mutual satisfaction is evidence in favor of the enforceability of your agreement, should that ever become an issue in a divorce. In sum, this is a healthy process that neither of you should shy away from.

As I stated earlier in this chapter, once the final agreement is reached, both of you need to wait at least seven days before signing. This mandatory waiting period ensures that neither party feels rushed or pressured into signing. After seven days, both parties can sign the agreement, making it legally binding.

CREATING A REALISTIC TIMELINE

Given the steps involved and the legal requirements, here is a suggested timeline for drafting a prenuptial agreement:

- **Six to twelve months before the wedding**: Initiate the conversation with your fiancé.
- **Three to six months before the wedding**: Hire separate lawyers. Attorneys will direct you to obtain records to begin financial disclosures and put a draft of the agreement together.
- **Two to six months before the wedding**: Attorneys will review and negotiate terms with their respective clients

and make necessary revisions and finalize the terms of the agreement.
- **One to two months before the wedding**: Start the seven-day waiting period. Sign the prenuptial agreement. Store the agreement in a safe place.

Now that you have a rough timeline in place, let's get into the nitty-gritty details of the agreement and what a prenuptial agreement can do for you. In the next chapter, we will explore the details of the agreement to have a fruitful conversation with your fiancé. This will ensure that both parties feel heard and respected throughout the process. With careful planning and open communication, you can navigate this journey together and build a strong foundation for your future.

5

THE TERMS OF THE PRENUP

In order for you to have a strong prenuptial agreement drafted, you must consider potential future scenarios that may never exist because your lawyer is crafting something based on your life and details only you might know. Since most lawyers cannot predict the future, being able to explain the life goals that you and your fiancé have and share will help the lawyer plan and draft terms in your agreement accordingly. So, in this chapter, we'll dive into the critical components that a prenuptial agreement can cover and discuss the importance of aligning these terms with your life goals and those of your fiancé. Understanding each other's aspirations and financial expectations is key to having a productive discussion about the prenup and ensuring that the agreement reflects both your needs and desires.

UNDERSTANDING EACH OTHER'S LIFE GOALS

Before drafting a prenuptial agreement, it's essential to have a clear understanding of your own life goals and those of your fiancé. This understanding forms the foundation of a strong and fair prenuptial agreement. Life goals are not static; they evolve as circumstances change and as you both grow individually and as a couple.

If having these types of conversations with your fiancé makes you feel uncomfortable in any way, you will have to push past those feelings. For one thing, you should be able to discuss these kinds of thoughts and feelings with the person you intend to spend the rest of your life with. Moreover, once spouses are married in California, they become fiduciaries of the other, and these are the same duties owed to business partners. If you think about your relationship as a long-term investment in each other, this helps put perspective on things you might want to see in a prenup. If you look at your fiancé as a business partner who you would not be willing to do business with, then perhaps you may want to rethink marriage.

Here are some key considerations to discuss with your fiancé:

1. **Personal and Professional Aspirations:** You will need to discuss your long-term career goals, ambitions, and how you envision your professional lives developing.
2. **Financial Stability and Independence:** Lay out all your financial goals, including savings, investments, and plans for financial security. You will also need to discuss how you plan to manage shared expenses during marriage.
3. **Family Planning**: Talk about your desires regarding having children, family

responsibilities, and how you plan to support each other after the birth of your children in terms of household chores and management as well as management of future children's day-to-day activities. You should also talk about parenting styles, involvement of relatives in your lives, and how financial support of your children will be divided. You may also want to discuss artificial reproductive technology in the event that you need to seek assistance because it can take a physical, psychological, and financial toll on couples.
4. **Lifestyle Choices**: Plan to discuss your preferences for living arrangements, travel, and other lifestyle choices that could impact your finances.

THE EVOLUTION OF LIFE GOALS

Life goals can shift significantly over time. Data from the U.S. Census Bureau and Pew Research Center highlight these changes. For example, financial stability and independence have become top priorities for young adults today. Higher education and the associated debt also play a significant role in shaping financial goals.

According to Jonathan Vespa's 2017 report "The Changing Economics and Demographics of Young Adulthood: 1975-2016," and Richard Fry's 2023 update from the Pew Research Center, young adults are reaching key life milestones later than in the past. Some of these milestones include completion of formal education and when young adults are buying their first houses and having children. In more recent years, young adults are putting off having children in order to prioritize education and financial stability. Some adults are realizing the importance of protecting assets for their children from prior marriages than they did in the past. These shifts emphasize the need for flexibility and understanding in your prenup discussions.

Here are some statistics to consider: As of 2021,

- Only 39 percent of twenty-one-year-olds were working full-time, compared to 64 percent in 1980.
- Financial independence among twenty-one-year-olds dropped to 25 percent compared to 1980 which means that their income was at least 150 percent of the poverty line, allowing them to live independently from their parents.
- Marriage and child-rearing are less common among young adults, with only 6 percent having children in the home at age twenty-one, and 22 percent entering marriage by age twenty-five.
- Higher education is a major life milestone, with 48 percent of twenty-one-year-olds being enrolled in college. However, this raises the issue of trade-offs for that education, including crushing student loan debt, real-life experience, and the ability to find jobs to pay off that debt. So, at this young age, marriage consideration is very low on the life goal scale, with less than 6 percent of people in this age group having children in the home at this

point. At twenty-five-years-old, marriage is still a less significant consideration, with 22 percent in this age group entering into marriage, but children in the home can be seen a little more, with 17 percent in this age group.

These statistics underline the importance of discussing and revisiting life goals regularly throughout your marriage, ensuring that your prenuptial agreement remains relevant and fair.

So, if you and your fiancé have a prenuptial agreement in your early thirties, by the time you are fifty, your financial landscape will have changed, especially if you had children between these ages. It is not that uncommon in recent years for men to stay at home and care for children especially when employment is transitional (e.g., layoffs or seasonal work). Perhaps you supported your spouse through a master's degree or doctorate or several promotions, in which case, her financial portfolio may have caught up to yours. In these examples, it will be possible for parties to amend their prenuptial agreement, as needed during marriage, or create a post-nuptial agreement that handles specific issues that fall outside of the scope of the terms in your prenuptial agreement.

KEY COMPONENTS OF A PRENUP

A well-crafted prenuptial agreement should address several critical areas to protect both parties and reflect your mutual understanding and agreements. Here are the main components.

Income and Asset Protection

In the State of California, upon marriage, absent a prenuptial agreement saying otherwise, everything that is acquired during marriage is presumed to be community property. This may include all forms of income and work efforts made to earn that income during the marriage. It can also include the appreciation or depreciation of community property assets. In the event of divorce, without a prenuptial agreement, community property is divided equally between the parties. This means that the home that you might purchase during marriage with your fiancé/spouse, absent an agreement saying otherwise, would be presumed to be a community property asset and the court would have the power to order that home to be sold to equally divide the equity in that home between the parties.

Absent a prenuptial agreement, separate property is any property that is acquired before marriage and after the date of separation. So, to the extent that you can trace any down payment used to purchase a home during marriage, you would be entitled to reimbursement without interest. This means that you would be reimbursed for your separate property down payment but that you would not be entitled to a percentage in equal ratio to the equity that accumulated because of that separate property contribution. Moreover, any separate property contribution would be similar to an interest-free loan to the community estate.

In a prenuptial agreement, you clearly identify where you would have separate property and what you intend to maintain as separate property. In essence, you would have a record of what you had in the beginning stages of your marriage, and should you never update your prenuptial agreement or obtain a post-nuptial agreement, you would have a record to demonstrate a tracing back to the source of your separate property should that separate property ever be sold or reinvested into different accounts. Additionally, you can opt out of a community property estate completely. You can limit your work efforts during your marriage to your separate property. You can dictate when and how you plan to create community property during your marriage.

A prenuptial agreement also provides for debt protection. As with assets, debts that are acquired during marriage are presumed to be community property, absent an agreement saying otherwise. Assigning debt as separate property during marriage can ensure that premarital debts remain the responsibility of the individual who incurred them. Therefore, you should include in your discussions with your fiancé, any existing debts, such as student loans or credit card balances, and how they will be managed during the marriage.

Inheritance and Gifts

Inheritance is generally characterized as separate property whenever it is acquired. However, you can use a prenuptial agreement to quantify and memorialize any inheritance or trust distributions you receive or have a reasonable expectation of receiving. When I say reasonable expectation of receiving, I am not talking about your parents telling you that they left you something in their will or trust and you will inherit from them in the event of their death. The inheritance must be to a point here it cannot be modified by the benefactor.

You will want to discuss gifts from family members. In most divorces, the family of one of the spouses will have offered funds to the former couple to purchase real property or invest in a business. A gift, absent an agreement saying otherwise, is the separate property of the spouse receiving the gift. But, if the gift from family members is not clearly specified as a gift to only one of the spouses, the court may presume that gift was given to both parties.

Premarital Cohabitation: Living Together before Marriage

Your prenuptial agreement will also address claims arising from cohabitation without marriage. While nonmarried persons have no duty to support the other, that does not prevent people from entering into contracts, both verbally and in writing, to acquire assets and debts together prior to marriage. Therefore, a prenuptial agreement can clarify each party's interest in premarital assets and debts.

Financial Support

During marriage, both spouses must financially support one another, but if there is a prenuptial agreement there is no guarantee that upon divorce a spouse would be entitled to spousal support. In California, spousal support is based on several factors, but primarily on the length of the marriage, the income of the parties at the time of divorce, the martial standard of living, and the ability to pay. In marriages over ten years duration, the courts in California could retain jurisdiction to award spousal support to either party for life or until remarriage of the supported spouse. Of course, if there is an agreement between divorcing parties or an order of the court to terminate its jurisdiction then it will lose jurisdiction. The point here is that leaving spousal support jurisdiction up to the court is a gamble. Therefore, you will want to clarify in your prenuptial agreement whether either of you might need spousal support. If yes, for how long and for how much based upon current and potential scenarios such as if either one of you is temporarily unable to work to care for children or due to periods of disability.

PREPARING FOR THE PRENUP DISCUSSION

You can't expect your lawyer to figure out what you want to do with your life. You and your fiancé should come to the table with a clear understanding of your goals and how you want to handle the issues that matter most to you. This preparation could involve using *The Prenup Workbook: A Different Kind of Marriage Planning* as an invaluable tool in guiding your discussions. It helps you list your assets, debts, and financial goals, and includes guided questions to facilitate meaningful conversations.

As previously stated, the discussion about your prenuptial agreement should not be a one-time event. Plan for multiple conversations to ensure that both of you feel heard and understood. You should be open to revisiting and revising your prenup as your life goals and circumstances change over time.

CONCLUSION

Creating a prenuptial agreement that truly reflects both partners' life goals and financial expectations is a process that requires time, understanding, and careful planning. By having open, honest discussions and using tools like *The Prenup Workbook*, you can ensure that your agreement addresses all critical areas and protects both parties' interests.

In the next chapter, we will delve into more detail about divorces in California and the practical aspects of drafting the prenup with your lawyer, focusing on the legal language, and how to ensure that your agreement is comprehensive and enforceable. With the right preparation and mindset, you can navigate this process smoothly and arrive at an agreement that strengthens your relationship and sets a solid foundation for your future together.

6

WHAT HAPPENS WHEN YOU DO NOT GET A PRENUP IN CALIFORNIA

Understanding the implications of not having a prenuptial agreement is crucial, especially in a community property state like California. In this chapter, we'll explore what happens during a divorce when there's no prenup in place, highlighting the potential financial consequences and the importance of protecting your assets.

THE LEGAL LANDSCAPE IN CALIFORNIA

California is a community property state, which means that any assets or debts acquired during the marriage are considered jointly owned by both spouses and are divided equally in the event of a divorce. This 50-50 split can have significant financial implications, especially if one spouse has accumulated substantial wealth or if there are complex financial assets involved.

Key Points about Community Property

Community property between spouses in California grants equal rights to ownership, control, and interest regardless of who earned the income or whose name is on the title of an asset. Community property includes assets, debts, and income. In the event of divorce, everything acquired during the marriage is subject to a community property characterization, and upon such a finding, the court will equally divide the asset or debt between the spouses.

In comparison, assets, income, and debts owned or acquired prior to the marriage, or acquired by gift or inheritance during the marriage, are considered separate property. Upon a finding of a separate property characterization by the court in the event of divorce, the asset is not subject to division. However, commingling these assets with marital assets can complicate matters and a potential transmutation of what would be a separate property asset into a community property asset. Additionally, the community estate could acquire an interest in your separate property during the marriage if the community made contributions towards the acquisition of the asset or in the increase in value of the property or account. In a similar vein, if separate property is used to pay down community property debt or to acquire something during the marriage, separate property may be reimbursed to the contributing spouse.

REAL-LIFE EXAMPLES OF FINANCIAL IMPACT

To illustrate the potential consequences of not having a

prenuptial agreement, let's look at some real-life examples from my experience as a divorce attorney.

Case 1: The High-Earner

My former client was a successful entrepreneur and employee of a large company. He got married without a prenup. Within six months of marriage, he realized that the relationship was not going to work. However, despite being married for only six months, his substantial income and investments during that period became community property.

At the time of divorce, it was discovered that he had made significant contributions to his investment and retirement accounts, such that he acquired approximately $120,000 in value in these accounts. At the same time, his ex-wife was a salaried employee and did not save or contribute to any investment or retirement accounts to the extent that he did. The court determined that all that interest was community property. As a result, he was required to pay approximately $60,000 to his ex-spouse due to income contributions to his investment and retirement accounts during the brief six months of marriage. This substantial payout was a direct result of not having a prenup to protect his assets and income.

Case 2: The Long-Term Marriage

A former client was married for almost thirty years. During marriage, both spouses accumulated significant retirement savings. They were both union-backed employees, and each employer provided hefty pensions.

Aside from a home they purchased together, they had no other significant assets.

During the marriage, the ex-wife became disabled, and for the later years of the marriage, my client was the primary income provider. The ex-wife was able to collect disability income along with early retirement distributions but because she retired prior to the age of sixty, her monthly retirement payout was significantly less than it would have been had she waited until after sixty-five years of age to collect.

At the time of divorce, these retirement assets and the marital home were characterized as community property as they were obtained during the marriage. The marital home was sold, and the proceeds of sale were divided 50-50. The retirement plans were also split 50-50. Given that the ex-wife retired early due to disability, the value of her retirement account was insubstantial. It was used to offset her interest in my client's retirement plan, but because he had worked diligently throughout the marriage and was the primary source of income for a long period of time, what he thought he was going to be living on into his retirement years, was basically cut in half.

For people who work at W-2 income-based jobs (as employees), so near to retirement, a division in assets like this drastically reduced my client's planned retirement income, significantly impacting their financial stability in retirement. This impact was so drastic that my client had to obtain another job after retirement just to meet his basic monthly needs. This was due not only to the fact that he had half of his retirement income, but because he was ordered to pay an amount of spousal support to his ex-wife after the court determined that his Social Security earnings and his retirement earnings were still substantially more that the ex-wife's income.

These examples underscore the importance of having a prenuptial agreement, especially in a state like California where community property laws can lead to significant financial consequences.

POTENTIAL FINANCIAL CONSEQUENCES OF DIVISION OF THE COMMUNITY ESTATE

Without a prenuptial agreement, you stand to lose a significant portion of your assets and income in a divorce. You could also be saddled with debt that you did not know about that was acquired by your ex-spouse.

Here are some potential financial consequences:

- **Real Estate**: Your home and any other real estate acquired during the marriage will be divided equally.
- **Investments**: Stocks, bonds, and other investment accounts will also be subject to a 50-50 split.
- **Business Interests**: If you own a business, its value accumulated during the marriage can be divided, potentially affecting your control and ownership.
- **Division of Debts**: Any debts incurred during the marriage, such as credit card debt or loans, will also be divided equally, regardless of who incurred them.
- **Spousal Support**: In California, spousal support is dependent on the length of the

marriage, the needs of the supported spouse, and in general, the marital standard of living. There are several other factors that are considered when determining a long-term spousal support order, but a temporary spousal support order can be made during the divorce in an amount that would meet or get as close to the monthly martial standard of living, assuming that the other spouse has the ability to pay it. In most cases spousal support duration can be for one half the length of the marriage. But in marriages of over ten years duration, there is a potential for the court to have the power to make or modify spousal support orders for the life of the parties, remarriage of the dependent spouse, or further order of the court. Without a prenup, you may be required to pay spousal support, in an amount and duration that can be a significant ongoing financial drain for you, especially if there is a substantial income disparity between spouses.

- **Retirement Savings**: Retirement accounts, such as 401(k) or pension plans, will be divided, impacting your financial security in retirement.
- **Inheritance and Gifts**: While inheritances and gifts are typically considered separate property, commingling these assets with marital assets can lead to complications and potential division.

PROTECTING YOUR ASSETS WITH A PRENUP

A prenuptial agreement can help protect your assets and outline the financial arrangements in the event of a divorce, providing clarity and security for both parties.

Here's how a prenup can safeguard your interests:

- **Define Separate Property**: Clearly distinguish between separate and marital property to protect assets acquired before the marriage.
- **Protect Business Interests**: Ensure that your business remains your separate property, protecting its value and your control.
- **Outline Debt Responsibility**: Specify how premarital and marital debts will be handled, protecting you from being liable for your spouse's debts.
- **Establish Spousal Support Terms**: Define the terms of spousal support, providing predictability and fairness.
- **Safeguard Inheritances**: Ensure that inheritances remain your separate property, even if they are received during the marriage.

PREPARING FOR THE FUTURE

Understanding the potential financial impact of divorce without a prenup is a powerful motivator to take proactive steps to protect your assets. By planning ahead and discussing your financial expectations with your fiancé, you can create a prenuptial agreement that provides security and clarity for both parties.

Below are some steps to take:

- **Initiate the Conversation**: As discussed in Chapter 3, start the conversation with your fiancé early and approach it with openness and mutual respect.
- **Hire Experienced Lawyers**: Each party should have their own lawyer to ensure that their interests are represented and protected.
- **Full Financial Disclosure**: Be transparent about your financial situation, including assets, debts, and future expectations.
- **Draft the Agreement:** Work with your lawyers to draft a comprehensive prenuptial agreement that addresses all key areas of concern.
- **Review and Revise**: Take the time to review the agreement carefully and make any necessary revisions to ensure that it is fair and balanced.

CONCLUSION

A prenuptial agreement is not just a legal document; it is a crucial tool for protecting your financial future and ensuring that both parties enter the marriage with clear expectations and mutual respect. In a community property state like California, the absence of a prenup can lead to significant financial losses and unforeseen obligations. By understanding the legal landscape and taking proactive steps to draft a prenuptial agreement, you can protect your assets, secure your financial future, and build a strong foundation for your marriage.

7

PROTECTING THE MONEY GIVEN TO YOU

Inheritance can be a significant aspect of your financial landscape, and ensuring the protected intent of the person who made the gift as well as the management and control over it through a prenuptial agreement is essential. In this chapter, we will explore the complexities of ensuring that inheritance remains your separate property and the steps you can take to determine if and how you would want to make a gift of your separate property to your martial estate. Failing to be diligent about how your separate property inheritance is managed and controlled could inadvertently turn separate property into community property. With a prenuptial agreement, you can create a mechanism to trace your inheritance and/or to control its use in the future.

THE IMPORTANCE OF INHERITANCE PROTECTION

For many people, the desire to create a prenuptial agreement often comes at the behest of parents. In my experience as a divorce attorney, approximately 80 percent of clients seeking a prenup do so at the urging of their parents, particularly when inheritance is involved. Parents may express concern about what would happen to you in the event of a divorce. If you are the recipient of trust proceeds from grandparents or other deceased relatives, your family will want to ensure that family assets remain protected. Additionally, parents often have their own sizeable assets that they intend to leave to their children. These could be real property, investment accounts, life insurance proceeds, and businesses. If you are assisting in the management of any of these things, parents will have concerns about the potential accumulation of your fiancé's interest in ownership after marriage. I have seen many divorcing couples drag their parents into their divorce as a result of gifts that they made to one or both of the parties during the marriage. I've also seen the family business dragged through litigation during divorce because any work efforts during marriage are considered community property. So, in the middle of a divorce, the attorneys will want to value any increase in interest in these businesses that can be traced to your work efforts.

KEY POINTS ABOUT INHERITANCE PROTECTION

Inheritance is considered separate property, meaning it is not subject to division in a divorce, as long as it remains distinct from marital assets. If inherited assets are mixed with marital assets, they can lose their separate property status and become subject to division.

Understanding Commingling

Commingling occurs when separate property and marital property are mixed together, making it difficult to distinguish between the two. If a divorce occurs relatively recently to an inherited gift of real property or funds, it will be fairly easy to trace these funds because you would be able to obtain documentation to demonstrate the gift. After the passage of significant periods of time, what would have been used as evidence of the gift is often lost or destroyed, and it will be very difficult to prove an inheritance unless you are a diligent record keeper. Potentially, this means holding on to records for years.

An inheritance may be used to pay for repairs or remodeling of the marital home during marriage, start a business, or may be reinvested into new accounts. With the passage of time, it can be very easy to lose track of where the inheritance came from. While married, many couples do not have a problem sharing their separate property with their spouse, but at the time of divorce the feelings are very different, and a spouse may request a reimbursement of their separate property. As commingling can happen intentionally, with the passage of time, this commingling can unintentionally transmute separate property into community property, as the person who is claiming a separate property reimbursement has the burden of proving it existed and that it was used for the benefit of the community.

UNDERSTANDING TRANSMUTATION

Again, transmutation occurs when property – either separate or community – is changed. To change the character of a spouse's property from separate to community it usually requires a writing to demonstrate intent. However, if you have no documentation to prove that the separate property existed you cannot be reimbursed from the community. Likewise, community property can be transmuted into separate property, but for the sake of this discussion, I will stick to the separate-to-community property transmutation issue.

Here are some examples of transmutation:

- **Bank Accounts:** If you deposit inherited money into a bank account opened during marriage, that inheritance may be transmuted into community property. The account is presumed to be community property, absent a prenuptial agreement, because it was opened during marriage. The funds that are deposited into the account during marriage are also presumed to be community property, unless you can show where the funds came from. If you cannot trace your separate property funds in and out of that account during marriage, you will have inadvertently given the community your separate property.
- **Real Estate**: Using inherited funds to pay the mortgage or make improvements on any real property home, condo, commercial property or apartment building during marriage could transmute those funds into community property, unless you can demonstrate where the funds came from to purchase the real property.

- **Income from Inherited Property**: If income generated from an inherited property is deposited into a bank account opened during marriage or used for community property living expenses, that income could be transmuted into community property.

CASE STUDIES ON INHERITANCE COMMINGLING AND TRANSMUTATION

To illustrate the impact of commingling, let's look at some real-life scenarios from my practice.

Case 1: The Shared Investment Account

Sarah inherited over $100,000 in stock in a publicly traded company from her father during marriage. Sara opened a brokerage account to hold that stock and to do some investing of her own. Over time, the stock from the company was sold and / or divided in a buyout / merger of the company. Sarah had no control over this transaction as she was just a minority shareholder in a publicly traded company. The company then became several different companies with different names. Now twenty years after the death of her father, Sarah is in the middle of her divorce and has no records to demonstrate the inheritance. Moreover, what she does have to demonstrate the gift is nothing more than a letter from her brokerage account showing the deposit of stock. As the brokerage account was opened during marriage, and the inherited stock was commingled with other stock that Sarah bought and traded during marriage, Sarah could not demonstrate the source of initial stock deposit, and the entire account and its stock are considered community property.

Case 2: The Family Home

John inherited $250,000 from his mother during marriage. He used part of those funds to renovate the home that he and his wife purchased during marriage. The renovations added significant value to the home. With the rest of the funds, he purchased a car for his wife. Seven years later, John is in the middle of a divorce from his wife. John was able to obtain copies of checks from his mother's estate to demonstrate that he received $250,000 as an inheritance. John is entitled to reimbursement of his inheritance, but no equity is apportioned to his contribution to the improvements made on the marital home. Nor is he entitled to interest. He is essentially deemed to have made an interest-free loan to the community. So, while he will get his monies back, he has lost out on interest that could have accumulated on those funds because he used them to improve community property instead of investing the funds elsewhere.

PROTECTING YOUR INHERITANCE

To safeguard your inheritance and prevent unintentional transmutation which could lead to a transmutation of your separate property, you need to take specific steps and include clear terms in your prenuptial agreement.

To protect your inheritance:

- **Separate Accounts**: Keep inherited funds in a separate bank account that is not used for marital expenses.
- **Accurate Record-Keeping**: Maintain detailed records of all transactions involving your inheritance, including deposits, withdrawals, and how the funds are used.
- **Legal Documentation**: Ensure that any inherited property is legally documented in your name only and avoid using marital funds for improvements or maintenance.
- **Clear Prenup Terms**: Include explicit terms in your prenuptial agreement that outline how inherited assets and any income generated from them will be handled.

DEALING WITH COMPLEX INHERITED ASSETS

Inheritance often involves more than just cash. You may inherit real property, insurance proceeds, or income-generating assets, each with its own set of challenges.

As to specific assets, here is some key information to prevent potential problems in the event of a divorce, while you have a prenuptial agreement in place.

Real Property

- **Title Changes**: Ensure that the title to any inherited real property is in your name alone and avoid adding your spouse's name to the deed.
- **Use of Property**: If you plan to use the inherited property for marital purposes, such

as living in an inherited house, be cautious of any improvements or expenses paid with martial income.

Insurance Proceeds

- **Timing of Payouts**: Insurance proceeds from the death of a loved one might not be paid out immediately. When received, deposit them into a separate account.
- **Investment of Proceeds**: If you invest the proceeds, ensure that the investments remain in your name only and are not commingled with marital funds.

Income Streams

- **Separate Accounts for Income**: Any income generated from inherited property, such as rent or dividends, should be deposited into a separate account.
- **Use of Income**: Avoid using this income for marital expenses to prevent creating a community property interest.

CONCLUSION

Protecting your inheritance requires careful planning and diligent financial management. By keeping inherited assets separate, maintaining accurate records, and clearly outlining terms in your prenuptial agreement, you can ensure that your inheritance remains your separate property. Understanding these issues and taking proactive steps will help you avoid commingling and unintentional transmutation and preserve the legacy intended for you by your loved ones.

8

THE HOUSE YOU BOUGHT BEFORE MARRIAGE

Owning a home or any real property before marriage is a significant investment and can become a complex issue during a divorce. Understanding how your separate property house can acquire a community property interest is crucial for protecting your investment. In this chapter, we will explore the intricacies of maintaining your separate property status and the steps you can take to safeguard your home and other real property through a prenuptial agreement.

THE NATURE OF SEPARATE PROPERTY

When you purchase a home before marriage, it is considered your separate property. This distinction is important because, in a community property state like California, assets acquired before the marriage are not subject to division upon divorce. To be clear, in the event of divorce in California, because the court has jurisdiction over you and your divorce, it will make orders to equalize the division of marital assets between you and your spouse using community property. But if there is an unequal division or funds need to be repaid to the community, it could order that your separate property be used to satisfy that debt.

Assuming that the initial investment used to purchase real property came from separate property sources, the money you used to purchase the home before marriage should be considered separate property. It is important to keep track of the value of the home and the initial contributions made toward the purchase of that home in the event of divorce because it could affect potential reimbursement claims of that separate property if the court determines that you transmuted your separate property home into community property. Some examples of separate property sources are income and savings earned prior to marriage, investments accounts (including some retirement accounts) and contributions into that account prior to marriage, income earned from assets that were acquired prior to marriage, and gifts made specifically to you from a traceable source, prior to marriage.

With the passage of time and years of marriage, you may sell your separate property home and acquire a new marital home. Again, in this case, absent a prenup, the new home would be considered community property, but you would be entitled to a dollar-for-dollar reimbursement of the separate property funds used to purchase the new marital home.

If you turn your separate property home into a rental property, assuming that you hire someone or a company to manage that property, the rent and income generated from that property would be considered community property. In that case, you would need to document and possibly safeguard those funds, if you want to claim a reimbursement in the event of divorce. Additionally, you could use the rental income to purchase more property. But again, if this is purchased during marriage the presumption is that the asset or property is community property, and you have the burden to prove your separate property interest.

During your marriage, maintaining the separate property status of your home will require careful financial management and legal protection because even if real property was acquired prior to marriage, and is titled in your name alone, the community estate may obtain an interest in the property during the marriage.

There are a few ways in which the community could acquire interest in your separate property real estate. If community property is used to pay down your separate property mortgage or make improvements to your separate property home, you may be creating a community interest in the home, absent a prenuptial agreement. If community property credit is used to refinance a separate property mortgage during marriage, you may also create a community property interest in the property.

A mere change in title alone may not transmute your separate property into community property. In California, transmutation of separate property to community property requires writing with key words indicative of intent in addition to a change in title. Even if intent is proven, because of the fiduciary relationship between spouses, a separate property reimbursement would be likely to avoid the appearance of undue influence.

If mortgage payments are made with community property funds (income earned during the marriage), this can create a community property interest in the home, even if the home is titled in your name alone. Additionally, improvements and maintenance paid for with community funds can also contribute to a community property interest, absent a prenuptial agreement. Therefore, even though you bought the house before marriage, the continued use of community property funds for your separate property during the marriage can provide your future spouse with the right to a percentage of equity in that home. In this case, you may have to refinance a mortgage to draw out equity to pay the community its share of equity in your home or sell the property if you have no other financial resources from which to pay the other party.

You may also transmute your interest in the real property from separate to community by doing a refinance of the mortgage on that property by using your spouse's credit to qualify for that loan, draw out equity, and place your future spouse's name on title. Some or all of these combined examples of events can collectively create a community interest in your property. In general, the proceeds of a loan taken out during marriage are community property and in the event of divorce, those proceeds need to be reimbursed to the community. Since the loan is tied to the property, the property may need to be sold to reimburse the community in addition to paying out any equity the community might have acquired because of that loan.

As a complex example, a former client refinanced several of her premarital rental properties in order to purchase a commercial building during marriage. She did not have enough in case to purchase the property outright and needed to take out a small loan to pay the balance. The property was titled in her name as her sole and separate property. The parties rented the property to their own business that they formed during marriage.

At the time of divorce, it was explained that the lender for that loan used the income of my former client and her soon-to-be ex-husband to qualify for the loan. The parties then used rental proceeds from the community property business that occupied the property to pay for the mortgage. As a result, the court made a finding that the commercial building was not my client's sole and separate property. Instead, she was entitled to a reimbursement of the funds used as a down payment, and the balance of interest in the building was community property.

In this example, because my client did not have a prenuptial agreement, she essentially made an interest-free loan to the community. While she did get additional interest in the property from her one-half share, her intent to keep the property as her own ultimately failed.

REIMBURSEMENT AND TRACING

Assuming that you transmuted your separate property home to community property, California law permits you the right to reimbursement of your separate property interest in the property so as to not unjustly enrich the community in a real property transmutation that was not intended. In this case, the community would owe you the reimbursement. However, reimbursement of separate property contributions to a community property asset requires meticulous record-keeping and clear evidence to demonstrate your separate property interest. You must remember that in community property states, the presumption is that anything obtained during marriage is community property. So, the burden to prove a separate property or separate property interest in any community property is on the person seeking the characterization or reimbursement. Depending on the circumstances, you may not be able to save that property and keep it as your separate property, especially if there is any order to liquidate assets to satisfy the court's order to equitably divide the value of the asset or repay the community.

If you did not transmute your interest in real property from separate to community property, as briefly expressed above, you may have still allowed the accumulation of a community property interest in the property in that the reimbursement is to the community in addition to the accumulated interest in ownership value (equity) for that contribution.

As we discussed in prior chapters, here are some key points about reimbursements owed to you from the community without a prenuptial agreement:

- **Dollar-for-Dollar Reimbursement**: You are entitled to reimbursement for your separate property contributions, but without any interest or appreciation.
- **Burden of Proof**: You must prove the amount of your separate property contributions to claim reimbursement.
- **No Interest on Contributions**: The reimbursement is limited to the exact amount contributed, without accounting for the increase in property value.

PROTECTING YOUR HOME WITH A PRENUP

Including specific provisions in your prenuptial agreement can protect your separate property interests and prevent the commingling of assets. Here's how you can safeguard your home:

- **Specify Ownership**: Clearly state that the home purchased before the marriage remains separate property.
- **Mortgage and Expenses**: Define how mortgage payments and home-related expenses will be handled to avoid community property contributions.
- **Reimbursement Provisions**: Include detailed reimbursement provisions for any community contributions made toward the property.
- **Separate Accounts:** Use separate accounts for any payments or improvements related to the home to maintain clear financial records.

By way of example, one of my clients was planning to get married to someone who had sizeable real property assets that he wanted to keep as his separate property. He had adult children from a prior relationship, and he wanted to make sure that his estate was given to his children in the event of his death. However, he wanted to create a mechanism during marriage to allow for the creation of some community property. My client also had a real property asset that she wanted to protect. Her fiancé was living off trust and dividend income from managed assets that were basically set on auto pilot, and he really had no management over the investments except for the occasional phone calls to his broker.

To keep things nice and neat, he specified in the prenup that he intended to purchase a real property home and take it in joint title with his fiancé, and that taking title in real property jointly would create community property, and that would be the only way in which community property was created. Because my client also had children of her own and her own estate, she agreed because she was able to secure her own assets for her children and if they decided, my client and her fiancé could own things together in the future.

CONCLUSION

Owning a home before marriage presents unique challenges in maintaining its separate property status. By understanding the implications of community property contributions and implementing clear provisions in your prenuptial agreement, you can protect your investment and avoid unintended financial consequences. Careful planning, meticulous record-keeping, and proactive legal measures are essential to safeguarding your assets.

9

REIMBURSEMENTS FOR STUFF PAID FOR BEFORE MARRIAGE

Understanding the financial liabilities and reimbursements related to expenses incurred before marriage is crucial for anyone considering a prenuptial agreement. In this chapter, we will delve into the legal principles surrounding property interests and liabilities between unmarried persons, and how these can impact your financial situation if not properly addressed in a prenup.

LIABILITIES BETWEEN UNMARRIED PERSONS

In California, when two individuals live together and share expenses with the intention of eventually marrying, financial entanglements can become complex. In California, the concept of "Marvin Actions" can come into play, named after the landmark case *Marvin v. Marvin*, which addressed property rights between unmarried cohabitants. This means that non-spouses do not have the same rights as spouses. California does not have common law marriage, which is marriage based on the length of time statutorily that a couple must reside together to be considered a legal spouse. The court may enforce contracts between non-spouses, not based on a sexual relationship, but the burden to prove the existence of a contract in the absence of a written one is heavy.

KEY POINTS ABOUT MARVIN ACTIONS

A Marvin Action is a claim that is usually made in civil court because family court is for married persons or persons with shared children. So, most Marvin claims are made in the event that unmarried people end their relationship. That doesn't mean that your spouse, in the event of a divorce, could not make a Marvin claim in the divorce proceedings. Marvin Actions recognizes that cohabiting partners may have implied contracts or agreements regarding property and financial support.

Courts can enforce these implied agreements, awarding property or financial support based on the understanding between the parties. An implied contract is not written or explicitly stated but is formed based on the conduct of the parties involved.

Here are some ways implied contracts can be recognized between non-spouses.

Joint Purchase of Property

As unmarried persons, if you and your partner purchase a property together, and both contribute to the mortgage payments, an implied contract may be formed regarding the ownership and division of the property, should the relationship end. In the event of divorce, the court must determine if an implied contract was created based on the conduct, actions, and verbal agreements of the parties. Evidence such as financial contributions, written communications, and witness testimonies can be crucial in establishing the existence of an implied contract.

The court will assess the contributions of each party to the purchase and maintenance of the property. This includes down payments, mortgage payments, property taxes, insurance, and any significant improvements or renovations. The court will try to determine the intent and understanding of both parties regarding the ownership and division of the property based on the evidence provided. This may involve looking at the reasons behind each party's contributions and whether there was a mutual expectation of shared ownership.

Once the court establishes that an implied contract exists and assesses the contributions, it will then determine a fair division of the property. This may involve awarding one party a financial interest in the property or ordering the sale of the property and dividing the proceeds according to each party's contributions and the implied agreement. If one party seeks reimbursement for specific expenses related to the property (e.g., mortgage payments or renovations), the court will consider whether these expenses were made with the expectation of repayment. If the court finds that there was an implied promise of reimbursement, it may order the other party to compensate for these expenses.

In one example, a former client purchased a home with her boyfriend. Her name was not put on title. Instead, they agreed that she would pay to furnish the home and pay for their basic utilities along with a portion of the mortgage. The intent was that they were going to live in this home during their marriage. The marriage, for various reasons, did not happen, and my client moved out of the property. The boyfriend stayed in the property and paid the mortgage. In this Marvin Action, my client was able to obtain funds from the ex-boyfriend in order to reimburse her for all the furniture that he kept along with the monies that she paid toward the mortgage based on their verbal agreement and evidence of intent to marry.

Shared Business Ventures

Engaging in a business venture together and sharing profits and losses can create an implied contract regarding the management and division of the business assets and earnings. As in the process for determining an implied contract for the joint purchase of real property, the court must examine the conduct of the parties. The court will scrutinize the nature of the relationship between the parties and their conduct during the business venture. This includes how the parties interacted, their roles in the business, and how they shared profits and losses.

The court will consider verbal agreements or understandings, as well as actions that indicate a mutual agreement. This could include how the business was run, who made decisions, and whether both parties acted in a way that suggested an equal partnership. It will consider the financial contributions of each party, such as initial investments, ongoing financial support, and personal labor or expertise contributed to the business. This assessment helps determine the extent to which each party is expected to benefit from the business. Any emails, text messages, business records, or other documentation that reflect the parties' intentions and agreements will be reviewed. The court will consider whether both parties intended to share the business profits and losses and if there was an expectation of mutual benefit. Even informal communications can provide evidence of an implied contract. If an implied contract is established, the court might award a financial share of the business to one party or divide the business assets and profits according to the contributions and implied agreements.

Investment in Fiancé's Career

Prior to marriage, if one partner supports the other through school or helps them start a business with the expectation of future financial benefits or a share in the earnings, this can be considered an implied contract. For example, one partner might work full-time to support the other's education or forego career opportunities, with the understanding that they will be reimbursed or share in the future earnings of the other person. In this case, the court will scrutinize the nature of the relationship between the parties and the contributions made by the supporting partner. This includes financial support, emotional support, and other forms of assistance provided to help the other partner advance their career. The court will consider any and all communications between the parties that might indicate a promise of reimbursement or a share of future earnings.

Promises of Financial Support

To be clear, there is no duty of support between unmarried persons. In the event of a breakup between unmarried persons, the court will not order spousal support. It might consider verbal promises of financial support, coupled with actions that reinforce these promises to determine whether there was an implied contract to care for one of the parties. The court may consider the duration of the relationship, the level of commitment, and the extent to which the parties acted as though they were married (e.g., shared finances, joint property ownership). It may consider the financial contributions made by each party, including direct financial support, payment of living expenses, and contributions toward significant costs such as education or career development or lack thereof for sustained care of the other person. Based on the evidence provided, the court may assess whether one party relied on the promises of financial support and whether this reliance resulted in a detriment to them. This could include giving up career opportunities, incurring debts, or making significant lifestyle changes based on the expectation of financial support. For example, if one partner promises to financially support the other in return for taking care of the household, and this arrangement continues for a significant period, a court might recognize this as an implied contract.

When it comes to shared living expenses incurred before marriage, such as rent, utilities, and groceries, the general rule is that there is no reimbursement. These expenses are typically seen as part of the mutual support and maintenance of the household.

Examples of non-reimbursable expenses are:

- **Rent**: Payments made toward rent for a shared apartment.
- **Utilities**: Costs for shared utilities like electricity, water, and internet.
- **Groceries**: Daily living expenses for food and household supplies.

Wedding Costs and Debts

Wedding costs can be a significant financial burden, and understanding how these expenses are handled in the event of a breakup or divorce is essential. If wedding expenses are paid on credit and there is no prenuptial agreement, the debt could potentially be considered a community debt once married.

That said, there is no reimbursement for wedding expenses, between the parties, if the marriage does not take place. If wedding expenses are paid on credit and the marriage occurs, those debts could be considered shared debt subject to the jurisdiction of the family court and the court, in the event of divorce, could find that both parties are equally responsible for repayment.

INCLUDING PROVISIONS IN YOUR PRENUP

To avoid the complications and financial uncertainties associated with shared expenses and debts incurred before marriage, it is essential to include specific provisions in your prenuptial agreement.

In most instances, there will be a provision inserted into your prenuptial agreement regarding Marvin Actions. You will want to make sure to include detailed terms in your prenup regarding reimbursement for any significant contributions made before the marriage. These types of issues typically arise when parties purchase a home prior to marriage with the intent of living in it after marriage. Additionally, outlining how shared living expenses prior to marriage are not reimbursable and how shared expenses will be handled after marriage can help to ensure both parties understand that there will be no reimbursement for these costs. You will also want to include how any pre-marriage debts will be treated, particularly those related to wedding expenses, and ensure there is an agreement on how to manage and repay these debts.

CONCLUSION

Addressing liabilities and reimbursements for expenses incurred before marriage is a vital aspect of financial planning and protection. By understanding the legal principles of Marvin Actions and clearly outlining terms in your prenuptial agreement, you can avoid potential disputes and ensure fair treatment of pre-marriage contributions and debts. Proper planning and legal foresight can help you navigate these complex issues and maintain financial harmony both before and after marriage.

10

PROTECTING YOUR INCOME AND RETIREMENT

In this chapter, we will delve into how your income and retirement assets can become entangled with community property interests during marriage. Understanding how to protect these assets is essential for anyone considering a prenuptial agreement. We will explore the complexities of bonuses, employer-sponsored retirement contributions, stock and options, and business interests, and provide strategies for safeguarding your financial future.

THE NATURE OF INCOME AND RETIREMENT ASSETS

Income and retirement assets accrued during marriage are typically considered community property in California. This includes not only your salary but also bonuses, stock options, and contributions to retirement accounts. It is possible that some of the deferred compensation you earned before marriage might vest during marriage. It is also possible that your deferred compensation and / or bonuses would be based on work efforts that you made in consideration of your career and work efforts prior to marriage. So, it can be really important to clarify what happens to this income and how it will be characterized to avoid any confusion or conflict in the event of a divorce. Properly managing these assets and clearly defining them in a prenuptial agreement can help protect your interests.

KEY POINTS ABOUT INCOME AND RETIREMENT ASSETS

In the event of divorce, it is common in California for the court to look at bonuses and retention bonuses in a couple of different ways. If the bonus is based on work performed during the marriage as opposed to after the date of separation, the bonus is considered community property. It will usually be considered as income available for support and used for that purpose. This means that it could get added into your income when the court considers child support or spousal support orders.

If it isn't considered as income available for support, then the court may consider it a divisible asset for which each spouse is entitled to 50-50. Things get tricky when there is a mix of separate property characterization and community property characterization. In most of those cases, experts are retained to value the deferred compensation and / or bonus. Upon vesting, depending on how that compensation is paid to you, you will either need to pay a percentage of the value of the deferred compensation or a set dollar amount. If the deferred compensation is paid to you in the same way in which you receive your wages and salary, then that income should be excluded from your income available to support, to the extent that the asset does not belong to you as your own separate property.

As to retirement plans, any portion of the retirement plan (your own contributions or employer contributions) that was earned during marriage will be considered community property in the event of divorce. The type of plan you have will determine when and how it is paid out to the other spouse upon divorce. For example, for accounts like 401(k) or IRAs, the value of the account is based on the contributions made during marriage and a percentage of those gross contributions are apportioned to any equity in the account.

If you have a significant amount of funds that were acquired in the account prior to marriage, your separate property is reimbursable to you from the date of marriage, plus the attributed share of accumulated and apportioned interest. The court will also give you credit for any contributions that you made to the account after the date of separation and the apportioned interest on those contributions.

The court does not typically allow for the transfer of stock in lieu of cash out. Instead, the court will order that the non-employee spouse receives the cash value of account based on their one-half of the community interest in the account. It is then rolled over into another similar account owned by the non-employee spouse, usually an IRA, so that neither spouse is taxed for a premature withdrawal. Each party will then be able to have the plan manager or financial advisor reinvest the funds in their own accounts.

A typical example of this in San Diego, where I am located, is in the case of a military servicemember. Most often they opt in to a 401(k) and upon twenty years of service are eligible for a military pension. In the event of divorce, the court, based on the evidence and / or expert testimony, determines the community's interest in both accounts. As discussed above, the plan is divided based on one-half of the accumulated community interest in the plan. A special order is drafted to divide the account and the non-military spouse will roll over their interest into their own IRA.

The military pension is divided by court order and submitted to the pension manager – Department of Finance and Accounting Services (DFAS). I'm not going to get into the order and what that is because it's not relevant to our discussion. The non-military servicemember spouse will receive their share of the pension upon the payout of the plan to the servicemember based on one-half of the number of years of military service while married over the years in career. There are some exceptions to this, but for the sake of demonstration, I am only referring to a standard retirement after twenty years of service. Included in this payment could be the calculation of a survivor benefit if that is elected prior to retirement of the servicemember. The point here is that a pension payment, potentially years after a divorce, is something most servicemembers do not want to do. This is especially true when that military servicemember is remarried.

This example does not just apply to military servicemembers. No one can predict what kind of retirement benefits you could accumulate over time. You may want to deposit more of a percentage of income into those accounts to prepare for retirement. Most people do not want to share up to one-half of their retirement accounts with a spouse that they were married to years prior. Moreover, your wise investment strategy and retirement planning go out the window when the income you thought you were going to have in retirement is cut down by half.

THE COMPLEXITY OF STOCK OPTIONS AND STOCK AGREEMENTS

As briefly explained above, stock options and agreements present unique challenges in determining whether they are separate or community property. The court will look at the date the stock was acquired and whether it was tied to efforts during the marriage.

Some examples of stock option issues are:

- **Grant Date vs. Vesting Date**: Stock options granted before marriage but vesting during the marriage can have both separate and community property components.
- **Stock Agreements Signed During Marriage**: If a stock agreement is signed during the marriage but the stock matures after separation, an expert may need to be hired to determine the community interest.

MANAGING YOUR ASSETS

To effectively protect your income and retirement assets, consider the following strategies:

- **Detailed Prenuptial Agreement**: Obviously you should consider getting a prenuptial agreement to address these concerns. It should clearly define what constitutes separate and community property.

In your prenuptial agreement, you can decide if you want to provide for any community property accumulation and / or the creation of community property accounts. You should be clear about what you intend with deferred compensation.

- **Segregate Accounts**: As stated in preceding chapters, it is recommended to keep separate property income and assets in distinct accounts to avoid commingling. I am not suggesting that you have no joint accounts to pay for shared expenses. I am suggesting that tracing is difficult when separate property funds are deposited into a shared account. So, if you have retirement income in pay status or you intend to make large contributions toward retirement accounts for retirement planning, you should be clear that (1) you do not want to share your retirement and (2) you may not want to add your spouse as a beneficiary of the survivor benefit.
- **Documentation**: Maintain thorough records of all assets and contributions, including dates and sources of funds. This poses some difficulty with the passage of time, but if you do your best to segregate funds into separate property accounts, it will be easier to trace.
- **Regular Reviews**: You may want to periodically review and update your prenuptial agreement to reflect changes in your financial situation. Some people choose to amend their prenuptial agreements after

the passage of significant time. You may want to do this in the event of changes in assets.

PROTECTING BUSINESS INTERESTS IN THE EVENT OF DIVORCE

The Nature of Business Interests

Business interests can be particularly complex when it comes to community property law in California. A business that you start before marriage, but which grows and increases in value during the marriage, can have both separate and community property components. Additionally, if you start a business during the marriage, it is generally considered community property, unless specified otherwise in a prenuptial agreement.

KEY POINTS ABOUT BUSINESS INTERESTS

Valuation

The value of the business at the time of marriage and at the time of divorce is critical. The increase in value during the marriage can be attributed to community efforts, making it partially community property. A valuation of any business is going to be required when the parties dispute not just the value of the business, but also the percentage of ownership interest between the community and separate property shares. The most difficult cases I have had to deal with are the smaller construction-related contractor businesses or cash-heavy businesses. The records are often not properly maintained, if they exist at all, and most of the time the other spouse is collecting a paycheck to write off family expenses or working for free. To hire an expert to prepare a report, evaluate records, and testify in court can easily cost upwards of $20,000.

Active vs. Passive Appreciation

Absent a prenuptial agreement, as to separate property businesses, active appreciation (due to efforts, skills, or contributions of either spouse) is typically considered community property. Passive appreciation (due to market forces or other external factors) is more likely to confirm separate property characterization of the business.

Compensation

The compensation you draw from the business and how it is categorized (salary vs. dividends, for instance) can also impact the division of the business asset.

PROTECTING YOUR BUSINESS INTERESTS

Detailed Prenuptial Agreement

Clearly define the ownership and division of business interests. Specify what percentage of the business is separate property and outline how any appreciation will be treated. Include provisions that account for future growth, work efforts, additional investments, and changes in the business structure.

Business Valuation Clause

You may want to include a business valuation clause that specifies how the business will be valued at the time of divorce, should you decide that you want to create a community property business or allow for a community property business interest. This can help avoid disputes and provide clarity on how the business interests will be divided.

Separate Property Agreements

Consider separate property agreements that further detail and protect your business interests. These agreements can be updated periodically to reflect the current state of the business and its value. If you have business partners, they may also want an agreement that your fiancé will not acquire rights in the business.

Buy-Sell Agreements

A buy-sell agreement with business partners can include provisions for handling a partner's divorce. This ensures that the business can continue operating smoothly without disruption from personal matters.

Segregate Business Finances

Keep personal and business finances separate to avoid commingling. This makes it easier to demonstrate which assets are separate property and which are community property.

HOW BUSINESS INTERESTS MIGHT LEAD TO RETIREMENT PLANNING

Business interests can be a significant part of your retirement planning. Many business owners rely on the sale of their business or ongoing income from the business as a major component of their retirement strategy.

Here's how.

Selling the Business

You may plan to sell the business when you retire, using the proceeds to fund your retirement. A prenuptial agreement can ensure that the value of the business is fairly divided or that you retain control over the sale and distribution of assets.

Ongoing Income

If you plan to continue receiving income from the business during retirement, a prenup can help protect this income from being divided as community property in the event of divorce.

Business Succession Planning

A well-crafted prenuptial agreement can also support your business succession plan, ensuring that your intended successors are not adversely affected by a divorce.

CONCLUSION

Protecting your income, retirement assets, and business interests is a crucial aspect of financial planning in a marriage. By understanding the potential community property interests and taking proactive steps through a well-crafted prenuptial agreement, you can safeguard your financial future. Clear documentation, separate accounts, regular reviews of your prenup, and specific provisions for business interests are essential to maintaining the integrity of your separate property. Whether you are an employee, a business owner, or both, careful planning can help ensure that your hard-earned assets remain protected.

11

A GIFT MAY NOT ALWAYS BE A GIFT

Gifts are often seen as simple gestures of love and appreciation, but their legal implications can be complex, especially in the context of marriage and divorce. This chapter delves into the intricacies of gift-giving before and during marriage, providing a comprehensive understanding of how these gifts can affect your financial standing in the event of a separation. By the end of this chapter, you will be better equipped to navigate these complexities and make informed decisions regarding prenuptial agreements.

DIFFERENTIATING GIFTS BEFORE AND DURING MARRIAGE

Gifts can play a pivotal role in both the courtship and marriage phases. However, the legal treatment of these gifts can differ significantly based on the timing and circumstances under which they were given. This section aims to clarify the distinctions between pre-marital and marital gifts, emphasizing their potential impact during divorce proceedings.

The Engagement Ring: A Conditional Gift

One of the most common and significant pre-marital gifts is the engagement ring. In California, the legal treatment of an engagement ring hinges on the concept of a "conditional gift." This means the ring is given with the expectation of marriage as the condition. If the marriage does not occur, the condition is unmet, and the donor may have the right to reclaim the ring.

Imagine a scenario where an engagement is called off. The emotional turmoil is compounded by the legal question of who retains ownership of the engagement ring. If the couple does not marry, the ring is typically returned to the donor. Conversely, once the marriage takes place, the ring is deemed a completed gift and becomes the recipient's separate property. This can be particularly contentious if the ring holds significant monetary or sentimental value, such as being a family heirloom. Addressing this explicitly in a prenuptial agreement can prevent future disputes.

GENERAL CONSIDERATIONS REGARDING GIFTS PRIOR TO MARRIAGE

Gifts given with conditions attached, such as a car or funds for a future joint venture, may need to be returned if the condition is unmet. Courts can enforce implied contracts between cohabiting partners, turning what seemed like outright gifts into contributions toward a shared enterprise. We discussed this previously under the

Marvin Action. This can complicate matters, especially if the relationship ends before the conditions are fulfilled. For instance, if one partner provides money for the other to start a business with the expectation of future marriage and shared success, and the relationship ends, the court may view this as an investment rather than a gift.

GIFTS BETWEEN MARRIED PERSONS

Once married, the distinction between gifts and property transfers becomes more nuanced, particularly under California's community property laws. Understanding how these laws apply to gifts can help couples protect their assets and ensure fair treatment in the event of a divorce

COMMUNITY PROPERTY VS. SEPARATE PROPERTY

In California, property acquired during the marriage is generally considered community property, meaning both spouses have an equal interest in it. However, gifts between spouses can be treated as separate property if there is clear intent and documentation to support this classification. For example, if one spouse gifts the other a valuable piece of jewelry and explicitly states it is a gift, supported by proper documentation, it remains the recipient's separate property. Examples of proper documentation could include the card that comes with the gift or any other written notification that the item is a gift such as an email or text message.

EXAMPLES OF GIFTS AND POTENTIAL RECLASSIFICATION

Large Financial Gifts

Large financial gifts from one spouse to the other, lacking clear documentation, may be deemed community property, particularly if the funds were used for marital purposes. Properly documenting such gifts and stating the intent for them to be separate property is crucial.

Real Estate Transfers

Real estate transfers between spouses require careful consideration of titling and documentation. If a property is re-titled in both spouses' names, it may become community property. To retain its status as separate property, it should be explicitly documented as a gift and titled solely in the recipient's name.

Business Interests

Gifting business interests can be particularly complex. If the business is a community property asset, transferring a portion to the other spouse may be seen as reallocating community property. Clear documentation and explicit statements that the transfer is a gift of separate property are essential.

Family Heirlooms

Family heirlooms gifted during the marriage can pose

unique challenges. If a spouse gifts an heirloom to their partner, it is crucial to document the intent for it to remain the recipient's separate property. However, if the heirloom is intended to stay within the family line, the prenuptial agreement should address its return in case of divorce.

Joint Gifts

Gifts given to both spouses by a third party, such as wedding gifts or inheritance, can complicate matters. Generally, such gifts are considered community property. To avoid disputes, clarify the ownership of these gifts in your prenuptial agreement or through clear documentation at the time of receipt.

COMMINGLING AND TRANSMUTATION

Commingling

When separate property, including gifts, is mixed with community property to the point of becoming indistinguishable, it risks being classified as community property. For instance, depositing a cash gift into a joint account used for household expenses can change its classification. Maintaining separate accounts and detailed records helps preserve the separate property status.

Transmutation

Spouses can change the nature of a gift through written agreements. For example, a written declaration that a gifted car is separate property can protect its status in a divorce. Such agreements must be explicit and clear to be legally binding.

FACTORS COURTS CONSIDER

Intent

The donor's intent is a key factor in determining whether a gift is separate or community property. Courts examine evidence such as statements, actions, and written agreements to discern intent.

Documentation

Clear documentation, including written agreements and explicit property titling, supports the classification of a gift as separate property. Detailed records and clear statements prevent misunderstandings and legal disputes.

Use and Treatment of the Gift

How a gift is used during the marriage impacts its classification. If a gift is used for the marital community's benefit, it might be seen as community property. For example, using a cash gift to fund a family vacation or household expenses can alter its status.

In the case, *Buie v. Neighbors*, the wife bought a Porsche for her husband using her separate property funds. At divorce, the husband claimed that the car was a gift to him, and it was, therefore, his separate property. Under California law, at the time, gifts "between the spouses of clothing, wearing apparel, jewelry, or other tangible articles of a personal nature that is used solely or principally by the spouse to whom the gift is made and that is not substantial in value taking into account the circumstances of the marriage" were the only gifts that were not subject to the rule that the husband needed a writing demonstrating his wife's intent was to give him, and only him, the car. The court found that the gift was not a gift to the husband, but it was a gift to the community. In essence then, the wife was only able to recover one-half of the then value of the car at divorce, not the entirety of her separate property funds.

PROTECTING GIFTS WITH A PRENUPTIAL AGREEMENT

To avoid situations where a gift may not be a gift you wish to lose in the event of divorce, you may include provisions in a prenuptial agreement that might define a gift, limit the dollar amount of a gift, or clearly identify gifts that the other person will receive in the event of divorce.

To ensure clarity and prevent disputes, include specific provisions about the treatment of gifts in your prenuptial agreement. Here are some strategies:

- **Detail the Treatment of Specific Gifts**: Explicitly state which gifts are to remain separate property.
- **Document the Intent**: Clearly document the intent behind each gift, supported by written agreements.
- **Keep Detailed Records**: Maintain detailed records of gifts and their use to

support their classification as separate property.
- **Consult Legal Experts**: Seek advice from legal experts to draft comprehensive prenuptial agreements that address potential future disputes regarding gifts.

By understanding and applying these principles, you can protect your assets and ensure a fair resolution in the event of a divorce.

CONCLUSION

Navigating the complexities of gift-giving in marriage requires careful consideration and planning. By understanding the differences between gifts given before and during marriage, and the implications of their treatment in divorce proceedings, you can make informed decisions about how to protect your financial interests. Including specific provisions in your prenuptial agreement regarding the treatment of gifts can provide clarity and peace of mind, ensuring a fair and equitable resolution in the event of divorce.

12

STAYING OUT OF YOUR FIANCÉ'S POTENTIAL LEGAL ISSUES

Protecting your future spouse from potential legal liabilities and risky business interests is crucial for maintaining financial security and marital harmony. In this chapter, we will explore strategies for safeguarding your partner from legal issues, including business liabilities and marital debts. By understanding these risks and taking proactive steps, you can create a solid foundation for your prenuptial agreement and ensure the financial well-being of both parties.

RECOGNIZING POTENTIAL LEGAL RISKS

Before entering into marriage, it's essential to identify and understand any potential legal risks that could impact your partner. From business liabilities to marital debts, various factors can expose your fiancé to legal issues that may affect both of you.

Business Liabilities

If your fiancé owns a business, they may be exposed to potential lawsuits or legal claims from clients or customers. For instance, a client could sue for injuries sustained on business premises, or a former employee might file a wrongful termination lawsuit. Moreover, there are some professions that do not allow for people who are not also in the same category of profession, like lawyers, to have any ownership interest in the business. Business partners may also engage in high-risk enterprises for the business, and if the business gets sued for business partner dealings, the community may be used to satisfy financial obligations and judgments.

Marital Debts

Unpaid debts, such as credit card debt or other liabilities, can become joint obligations during marriage, putting both parties at risk. Even if the debt was incurred by one spouse, it might still affect the couple's financial stability. Creditors may enforce on property held in joint names. This means that they can collect from assets that are presumed to be community property.

Example Scenario

Mary is a personal trainer and owns her own fitness studio. During her marriage to John, one of Mary's clients sues her for an injury sustained during a training session. In the event of a lawsuit, the community property may be liable for any damages awarded to the plaintiff. Without proper protection, John's assets could be at risk, even though he was not directly involved in Mary's business.

TIMING OF LEGAL BATTLES AND DIVORCE

It's crucial to consider the timing of legal battles and potential divorce proceedings. Getting divorced in the midst of a significant legal dispute can complicate matters and leave assets vulnerable to creditors. Moreover, filing for bankruptcy during a divorce will prolong the divorce and potentially leave you liable for community debts that your ex-spouse could liquidate.

Assets acquired during marriage may still be subject to attachment by creditors, even after divorce proceedings have begun. This can complicate the division of property and potentially reduce the financial resources available to both parties post-divorce. Furthermore, divorcing during a legal battle may raise suspicions of intent to defraud creditors, leading to additional legal complications. Courts scrutinize such actions, and attempting to shield assets this way can backfire.

MITIGATING RISKS THROUGH PRENUPTIAL AGREEMENTS

A well-crafted prenuptial agreement can help mitigate potential lawsuits and liability to creditors for debts incurred during marriage. By addressing business interests, marital debts, and legal timing in the prenup, you can create a framework for financial protection and stability.

Business Liability Provisions

In your prenuptial agreement, you may want to specify how business liabilities will be handled in the event of a legal dispute, including whether the community property will be at risk. This might involve stipulating that any business-related debts or liabilities remain the responsibility of the business owner alone.

Debt Allocation Provisions

You might want to clearly define how marital debts will be allocated and whether both parties will be responsible for unpaid debts incurred during the marriage. This can include provisions that each spouse is responsible for their individual debts and a detailed plan for handling joint debts.

Potential Lawsuits and Liability to Creditors Provisions

You may also want to include provisions addressing the timing of divorce proceedings in relation to ongoing legal battles, ensuring transparency and fairness. This can prevent the perception of fraudulent behavior and protect both parties' interests.

STRATEGIES FOR PROTECTING BUSINESS INTERESTS

For individuals with substantial business interests, it is crucial to incorporate specific strategies into the prenuptial agreement to protect these assets. This involves a combination of legal mechanisms and financial planning. The suggestions below are ways, in addition to obtaining a prenuptial agreement, in which you can shield your assets from lawsuit attachment if your business or their business is ever sued.

Separate Entity Formation

It is important that you and / or your fiancé think about establishing your business as a separate legal entity (e.g., LLC, corporation). Keeping business and personal assets separate and conducting business in this manner can help shield personal assets from business liabilities. You will want to consult with a tax professional and an attorney who specializes in business formations as to which type of business entity is right for you or your fiancé / future spouse.

Clear Ownership Agreements

This issue ties into the separate entity formation in that, whether or not there are business partners, the assets, debts, and liabilities should be referenced in the prenuptial agreement to the extent that they exist. I am not merely talking about an Operating Agreement for the formation of an LLC. I am talking about making sure that your prenuptial agreement identifies specific accounts, assets, and debts of the business to make it clear as to when things were obtained as well as how they relate to ownership and responsibility agreements within the prenuptial agreement. This will help to ensure that business interests are protected and that there is no ambiguity regarding each party's rights and obligations.

PROTECTING AGAINST MARITAL DEBTS

Marital debts can pose significant risks to financial stability, and a prenuptial agreement should address these concerns comprehensively. By clearly defining responsibility for debts acquired during marriage and establishing mechanisms for debt management, couples can avoid financial pitfalls.

KEY CONSIDERATIONS FOR DEBT PROTECTION

Pre-Marital Debt Clauses

In your prenuptial agreement, you should clearly state that each party is responsible for their pre-marital debts, ensuring that these liabilities do not become joint obligations. They should be specifically identified in your agreement to help trace the debt should that ever become an issue.

Debt Incurrence Policies

Your prenuptial agreement should establish policies for incurring new debts during the marriage, including joint decision-making processes and limits on joint liabilities. This will obviously depend on whether or not you intend to create any community property during your marriage, and how you will handle creditors and creditor communication should you decide not to create community property during your marriage.

Emergency Funds

You could consider creating an emergency fund and adding such a clause to your prenuptial agreement. The purpose of the funds would be to cover unexpected debts or liabilities during marriage or even after separation as part of a potential divorce settlement clause. It could provide financial security and prevent the need to rely on joint assets.

Example: Legal Mitigation through Prenups

Sarah owns a successful catering business. In her prenup with David, they agree that any liabilities arising from Sarah's business will be her sole responsibility, protecting David's assets from potential legal claims. The prenup provides clarity and protection for both parties, ensuring that David's assets are safeguarded in the event of legal issues related to Sarah's business.

Example: Debt Allocation

James and Emily include provisions in their prenup specifying that each party will be responsible for their respective pre-marriage debts. They also agree that any debts incurred during the marriage will be divided based on their individual contribution. In this example, a prenup helps allocate financial responsibilities fairly, reducing the risk of disputes over marital debts and providing a clear framework for financial management.

ADDITIONAL STRATEGIES FOR LEGAL RISK MANAGEMENT

Beyond the core elements of prenuptial agreements, there are additional strategies couples can employ to manage legal risks effectively. These strategies can provide extra layers of protection and ensure that both parties are well-prepared for any potential legal challenges.

Insurance Policies

Insurance policies can be identified in your prenuptial agreement.

Liability Insurance

You may want to consider obtaining liability insurance policies that can cover potential legal claims arising from business operations or personal actions. This insurance can provide financial protection and peace of mind, knowing that you have coverage in case of lawsuits.

Umbrella Insurance

Umbrella insurance policies offer additional liability coverage beyond the limits of standard insurance policies. This can be particularly useful for high-net-worth individuals or those with significant assets at risk.

Legal and Financial Advisors

You should schedule regular consultations with legal and financial advisors to review and update your prenuptial agreement and overall financial strategy. Advisors can provide valuable insights and help identify potential risks that may have been overlooked.

Tax Planning

Work with tax professionals to develop a tax-efficient strategy for managing business and personal finances. Proper tax planning can help minimize liabilities and ensure compliance with relevant laws and regulations.

CONCLUSION

Protecting your fiancé from potential legal issues is a crucial aspect of creating a comprehensive prenuptial agreement. By understanding the risks associated with business liabilities, marital debts, and legal timing, you can take proactive steps to safeguard both parties' financial interests. Including specific provisions in your prenup addressing these concerns can provide clarity and peace of mind, ensuring a strong foundation for your marriage.

13

CHILDREN AND CHILD SUPPORT

Understanding the legal landscape surrounding children and child support is essential for anyone considering a prenuptial agreement. In this chapter, we will explore the limitations and considerations when addressing future children and child support in your prenup. By gaining insight into the legal framework and public policy, you can approach discussions with your lawyer and fiancé with clarity and realistic expectations.

LEGAL CONSIDERATIONS ON FUTURE CHILDREN

When it comes to prenuptial agreements, there are significant limitations on what terms can be included regarding future children. Public policy dictates that custody and support arrangements for unknown or unborn children cannot be predetermined in a prenup. This is because the best interests of the child must always be the primary consideration for the courts, and these interests can only be assessed at the time of the custody or support proceedings.

Public Policy Constraints

Courts are reluctant to enforce prenuptial agreements that dictate custody or support arrangements for children who are not yet born. The reasoning behind this is that circumstances change, and it is impossible to predict what will be in the best interests of a child before they are even conceived.

Best Interests of the Child

Courts prioritize the best interests of the child when determining custody and support arrangements. This means that any provisions in a prenup that attempt to limit or predetermine these arrangements are unlikely to be enforced. For instance, if a prenup includes a clause stating that one parent will have sole custody of any future children, the court will not uphold this clause if it does not serve the best interests of the child at the time of divorce.

If you already have children with your fiancé, a provision in your prenuptial agreement as to custodial arrangements upon divorce is likely to be subject to amendment by the court in later court proceedings. Without getting into the weeds on child custody and visitation, courts are likely to enforce agreements between parents so long as they reflect the present circumstances between the parties and are in the best interests of the children. The court will not enforce any contractual effort to prevent either party from modifying child custody and visitation orders in the future. Until the children are eighteen years old and graduate from high school or nineteen years old (whichever occurs first), the court can modify any child custody and visitation orders that are consistent with their best interests and a demonstration of a change of circumstances.

Flexibility for Changing Circumstances

Furthermore, given the dynamic nature of life, it is crucial to have flexibility in legal agreements involving children. A prenuptial agreement cannot anticipate changes in financial status, health, or living conditions that might affect the best interests of a child.

PUBLIC POLICY ON CHILD SUPPORT

Child support is governed by public policy aimed at ensuring the financial well-being of children. While parties can agree on certain financial arrangements in a prenup, courts retain the authority to intervene if those arrangements conflict with public policy or the best interests of the child.

CHILDREN AND THEIR FINANCIAL SUPPORT

Legal Obligation

In California, both parents have a legal obligation to support their children financially, regardless of any agreements made in a prenup. This obligation cannot be waived or diminished by a prenuptial agreement. For example, a prenup cannot state that one parent will not have to pay child support to both living and future children, as this would be against public policy.

Court Intervention

Courts have the authority to set aside prenup provisions that conflict with public policy or fail to adequately provide for the needs of the child. This means that even if both parties agree to certain financial terms regarding child support, the court can override these terms if they are not in the child's best interest. The primary goal of child support is to ensure that the child's needs are met. Courts will examine all relevant factors, including each parent's income, the child's needs, and the standard of living the child would have enjoyed if the marriage had not ended.

Limits on Income Considerations

While prenuptial agreements may address financial matters, including income, there are limits to what the court can consider as income for child support purposes. Courts may set aside prenup provisions that attempt to restrict income for child support calculations. They have discretion to determine what constitutes income available for child support purposes. Courts must prioritize the financial well-being of children. This means that any attempt to cap or limit income for child support purposes in a prenup will likely be disregarded by the court. This can include not only actual earnings, but also potential earnings based on a parent's earning capacity. For example, if a parent voluntarily reduces their income, the court may impute income based on what they could reasonably be expected to earn.

Imputation of Income

Imputing income means assigning an income value to a parent based on their capacity to earn, rather than their actual earnings. The court can consider income from all sources minus business expenses to calculate a reasonable amount of child support. This ensures that parents cannot avoid their child support obligations by deliberately earning less.

REALISTIC EXPECTATIONS AND DISCUSSIONS

Given the legal constraints and public policy considerations surrounding children and child support, it's essential to approach discussions with realistic expectations. While prenuptial agreements can address financial matters, they cannot override the legal obligations and public policy considerations related to children.

Some guidelines for discussions with your fiancé are:

- **Open Communication**: Have open and honest discussions with your fiancé about expectations regarding children and child support. It is important to be clear about your financial situation and your views on supporting future children.
- **Legal Guidance**: Seek guidance from a qualified family law attorney to understand the legal implications and limitations surrounding children and prenuptial

agreements. An attorney can provide valuable insights into what can and cannot be included in your prenup.
- **Realistic Expectations**: Understand that while prenups can address financial matters, they cannot restrict or predetermine custody or support arrangements for future children. Recognize the importance of the best interests of the child standard and how it influences court decisions.
- **Flexibility and Planning**: Plan for flexibility in your prenup to accommodate future changes. This might include setting aside funds for potential child support or establishing guidelines for cooperative parenting.

THE ROLE OF COURTS IN CHILD SUPPORT AND CUSTODY

Courts play a crucial role in ensuring that child support and custody arrangements serve the best interests of the child. They have the authority to review and modify agreements to ensure that they meet legal standards and adequately provide for the child's needs.

Child Support Calculations

- **Income Assessment:** Courts will assess both parents' incomes to determine the appropriate amount of child support. This includes wages, bonuses, dividends, and any other sources of income. Courts may also

consider a parent's potential earning capacity if they are underemployed or voluntarily unemployed.
- **Child's Needs**: The court will evaluate the timeshare that each parent spends with the child at the time of divorce. The court may also consider the child's needs, including education, healthcare, extracurricular activities, and general living expenses. The goal is to maintain the child's standard of living as much as possible.
- **Parental Contributions**: Each parent's financial contributions and responsibilities will be considered. The parent with higher income or greater financial resources may be required to pay more in child support to ensure the child's needs are met.

Custody Arrangements

In the event of divorce, I have had many clients reach agreements as to how they want to share time with their children. I have also had many clients who have had to go to court to fight for time with their children. In one rare case, the court ordered that two of four siblings were to be split between their parents. Meaning, Child A primarily lived with the father and Child B never wanted to live with the father. The other two children would go back and forth between their mother and father. This meant that Child B would never spend time with Child A during much of the year, and the court felt this was a good idea based on the recommendations of an attorney who was appointed to represent the children, the level of conflict in the case, the ages of Child A and B, and their wishes. No matter which way parties end up with a court order, the court wants to make sure that children spend as much time with both of their parents in light of their health and safety.

Some other considerations the court will take into account are:

- **Best Interests of the Child**: When determining custody arrangements, the court's primary consideration is the best interests of the child. Factors include the child's relationship with each parent, the child's health and safety, and the ability of each parent to provide a stable environment.
- **Parenting Plans**: Courts encourage parents to develop parenting plans that outline custody and visitation schedules, decision-making responsibilities, and conflict-resolution mechanisms. These plans should prioritize the child's needs and foster a cooperative co-parenting relationship.
- **Modifications**: Custody arrangements can be modified if there are significant changes in circumstances, such as a parent's relocation, changes in the child's needs, or shifts in the parents' work schedules. Courts will review modifications to ensure they continue to serve the child's best interests.

PRACTICAL TIPS FOR DISCUSSING CHILD SUPPORT AND CUSTODY IN PRENUPS

While prenuptial agreements cannot predetermine child support and custody, they can still play a role in outlining expectations and fostering communication between partners. Here are some practical tips for addressing these topics.

1. **Be Transparent**: Share your financial situation, including debts, assets, and income, with your fiancé. Transparency helps build trust and allows for more informed decision-making.
2. **Focus on the Child's Best Interests**: Always prioritize the well-being of any future children in your discussions. Recognize that the court will make decisions based on what is best for the child, at the time of divorce, and not necessarily what is most convenient for the parents.
3. **Include General Guidelines**: While you cannot set specific terms for child support and custody, you can include general guidelines about co-parenting principles, such as a commitment to shared decision-making and fostering a positive relationship with the child. To be clear, guidelines are not contractual clauses but go to the intent of the parties.
4. **Plan for Financial Security**: Discuss setting aside funds for future child-related expenses, such as education or healthcare.

This can provide a safety net and demonstrate a commitment to the child's well-being.
5. **Seek Legal Advice**: Work with a family law attorney to ensure your prenup is legally sound and reflects realistic expectations. An attorney can help you navigate the complexities of family law and draft a comprehensive agreement.

CONCLUSION

Navigating the complexities of children and child support in the context of prenuptial agreements requires careful consideration and realistic expectations. By understanding the legal framework, public policy constraints, and limits on income considerations, you can approach discussions with clarity and informed decision-making. While prenups can provide valuable protection for financial interests, it's essential to recognize their limitations regarding children and child support and to engage in open communication with your fiancé and legal counsel.

14

SPOUSAL SUPPORT

Addressing spousal support, also known as alimony or maintenance, is a critical aspect of creating a comprehensive prenuptial agreement. In this chapter, we will explore the considerations, limitations, and strategies for including spousal support provisions in your prenup. By understanding the nuances of spousal support and crafting appropriate provisions, you can protect your financial interests while ensuring fairness and equity for both parties.

UNDERSTANDING SPOUSAL SUPPORT PROVISIONS

Spousal support provisions in prenuptial agreements can vary widely depending on factors such as income disparity, earning capacity, and the duration of the marriage. While it's possible to include limitations or waivers of spousal support, it's essential to consider the legal implications and potential challenges associated with such provisions.

Spousal support provisions are often influenced by the income disparity between spouses at the time of signing the agreement. For instance, if one spouse earns significantly more than the other, the lower-earning spouse may require financial support to maintain their standard of living post-divorce. Provisions that completely waive spousal support may be subject to challenge in future divorce proceedings, particularly if they result in significant financial hardship for the disadvantaged spouse. Courts scrutinize such waivers to ensure they are fair and that both parties fully understood the implications when they signed the agreement.

Courts strive to ensure that spousal support provisions do not leave one party in a financially precarious position while also considering the marital standard of living and ability to pay. Any agreement should reflect a balance that protects both parties' financial security and acknowledges the contributions and sacrifices made during the marriage.

STRATEGIES FOR CRAFTING SPOUSAL SUPPORT PROVISIONS

Crafting spousal support provisions that are fair, reasonable, and legally enforceable requires careful consideration and planning. By taking into account factors such as income, earning capacity, and the duration of the marriage, you can create provisions that provide financial security while minimizing the risk of legal challenges.

CONSIDERATIONS FOR SPOUSAL SUPPORT PROVISIONS

Income Disparity

If there is a significant income disparity between spouses at the time of marriage, consider offering some amount of spousal support to ensure fairness and equity. For example, a provision could stipulate that the higher-earning spouse will provide a specific amount or percentage of their income to the lower-earning spouse for a certain period post-divorce.

Full and Complete Waiver

While it may be tempting to include a full waiver of spousal support, consider the potential consequences and legal challenges associated with such provisions. Courts may set aside waivers that are deemed unfair or if the disadvantaged spouse did not fully comprehend the waiver's implications. That said, if you and your fiancé are on equal financial footing, you will want to make sure that your prenuptial agreement includes a spousal support clause that includes information about your earning and earning capacity at the time of signing the agreement.

Duration and Amount

It is recommended that a prenuptial agreement specifies the duration and amount of spousal support, taking into account factors such as the length of the marriage and the earning capacity of each spouse. This could involve setting a fixed monthly payment for a certain number of years or until the recipient spouse becomes self-sufficient.

In California, the duration of spousal support is based on the length of the marriage. For marriages of more than ten years duration, in the absence of a prenuptial agreement, the court could maintain the power to make spousal support orders for the life of the spouse in need. For marriages of less than ten years duration, the court has the power to order spousal support payments for one-half the length of the marriage. In marriages where there are large income disparities, this could mean you could be ordered to pay a large spousal support award for many years. That amount will be dependent upon the needs of the dependent spouse, the marital standard of living, your ability to pay it, and several other factors which include time out of the workforce to devote to the care and maintenance of the home and children. You can see why a spousal support clause in a California prenuptial agreement is important to include.

EXAMPLES: CRAFTING EFFECTIVE SPOUSAL SUPPORT PROVISIONS (DURATION AND AMOUNT)

James is a doctor and Emily is a firefighter. They specify in their prenup that spousal support will be provided to Emily for a period of three years following divorce, with the amount determined based on a percentage of James's income, which is defined in the agreement. In this example, both parties are working, and while James may earn more than Emily at the time of the prenuptial agreement, Emily has significant health and retirement benefits that outweigh James'. So long as the duration and amount of spousal support are clearly defined, it makes clear that the parties considered spousal support when negotiating the terms of their agreement. This arrangement allows Emily time to adjust and become financially independent while ensuring James's obligations are reasonable and time-limited. It can also allow James to make a lump sum buyout of support in the event that the parties ever get divorced. This means that James could add up all the amounts of support over the thirty-six months and pay Emily all at once. This may be something that Emily would prefer as well, especially when trying to move on at the time of divorce.

LEGAL CONSIDERATIONS AND CHALLENGES

Voluntariness and Disclosure

For spousal support provisions to be enforceable, both parties must enter the agreement voluntarily and with full disclosure of their financial circumstances. Any indication of coercion or lack of transparency can render the prenup invalid.

Unconscionability

Courts may refuse to enforce spousal support waivers that are unconscionable at the time of enforcement. This means that if enforcing a waiver of spousal support would result in undue hardship for one spouse, the court might modify or nullify the provision.

Judicial Review

Even with a well-crafted prenup, judicial review is a safeguard to ensure fairness. Courts retain the authority to adjust spousal support provisions if they find them to be unfair or not in line with state laws at the time of divorce.

CRAFTING SPOUSAL SUPPORT PROVISIONS

When considering the terms of your prenup regarding spousal support, you are forced to anticipate future changes. You will need to consider potential changes in circumstances, such as career advancements, health issues, or changes in living conditions. Including clauses that allow for modifications based on significant life changes can add flexibility and fairness to the agreement.

You should define clear conditions under which spousal support will commence, continue, or terminate. For example, support might end upon the recipient's remarriage or cohabitation with a new partner, or it might decrease if the recipient gains substantial employment.

You can also include a clause that requires mediation before any court proceedings. This can help resolve conflicts efficiently and with less animosity.

It is extremely important to consult with a family law attorney to ensure that your spousal support provisions comply with state laws and are likely to be upheld in court. An attorney can help draft language that is clear, fair, and enforceable.

You should also work with a financial advisor and / or accountant to understand the long-term implications of spousal support provisions. This includes considering the tax implications and how spousal support payments will affect your overall financial plan.

THE ROLE OF COURTS IN SPOUSAL SUPPORT

Courts play a critical role in ensuring that spousal support arrangements are fair and equitable. They may review prenuptial agreements, if the terms are ever challenged at the time of divorce, to determine if the provisions for spousal support align with legal standards and do not unfairly disadvantage either party.

In most cases, the court will enforce the terms of the prenup as they are written, but if there is a challenge to your prenuptial agreement during a divorce proceeding, the court will review the prenuptial agreement to assess its validity. This includes examining whether both parties entered into the agreement voluntarily and with full disclosure of their financial situations. The court will then evaluate whether the spousal support provisions are fair and reasonable. If the court finds that the provisions are heavily skewed in favor of one spouse, it may adjust the terms to ensure fairness. In the event that the court finds the terms of your prenup to be unconscionable, the court has the authority to adjust spousal support provisions if there have been significant changes in circumstances since the signing of the prenuptial agreement. Such significant changes would be changes in income, health, or other factors that affect the financial needs and capabilities of either spouse and the prenup was crafted with a full and complete spousal support waiver.

ENFORCEMENT OF SPOUSAL SUPPORT PROVISIONS

For spousal support provisions to be enforceable, they must comply with state laws and not violate public policy. Provisions that attempt to completely waive spousal support may face significant challenges, particularly if they result in one spouse facing financial hardship.

PRACTICAL TIPS FOR INCLUDING SPOUSAL SUPPORT IN PRENUPS

1. **Thorough Financial Disclosure**: Ensure that both parties provide a full and accurate disclosure of their financial situations when drafting the prenuptial agreement. This transparency is crucial for the agreement's validity and enforceability. The more information provided to the other party the better. For example, should you disclose your actual tax returns over a blanket statement in your prenuptial agreement as to your income and sources of income, it would add to the fact that there was a knowing and intelligent waiver of any right under the agreement.
2. **Consider Future Earning Potential**: Take into account not only current incomes but also future earning potential. This is particularly important if one spouse is expected to have a significant increase in

income due to career advancements or other factors.

3. **Plan for Different Scenarios**: Include provisions that address various potential future scenarios. For example, you might include different levels of spousal support depending on the length of the marriage or whether there are children involved.
4. **Be Fair and Reasonable**: Ensure that the spousal support provisions are fair to both parties. An agreement that is overly biased in favor of one spouse is more likely to be challenged and set aside by the court.
5. **Regularly Review and Update**: Periodically review and update the prenuptial agreement to reflect any changes in your financial situation or personal circumstances. This can help maintain the agreement's relevance and enforceability over time.
6. **Seek Professional Guidance**: Work with experienced legal and financial professionals to draft, review, and update your prenuptial agreement. Their expertise can help you create provisions that are both fair and legally sound.

CONCLUSION

Addressing spousal support in your prenuptial agreement requires careful consideration of factors such as income disparity, earning capacity, and the duration of the marriage. While it's possible to include limitations or waivers of spousal support, it's essential to do so in a manner that is fair, reasonable, and legally enforceable. By crafting effective spousal support provisions that provide financial security while minimizing legal risks, you can create a prenup that serves the interests of both parties and promotes marital harmony.

HOW TO BREAK THE NEWS THAT YOU WANT A PRENUP

Breaking the news that you want a prenuptial agreement can be a delicate and potentially challenging conversation to navigate. In this chapter, we will explore lawyer tips for expressing your desire to get a prenup effectively, fostering open and honest communication with your fiancé. By following these strategies, you can approach the discussion with confidence and create a safe space for meaningful dialogue.

UNDERSTANDING THE RISKS AND REWARDS

Engaging in discussions about a prenup carries the risk of uncovering potential differences or disagreements between partners. However, it also presents an opportunity for open and honest communication, which is essential for building a strong and lasting relationship. By approaching the conversation with empathy, respect, and a willingness to listen, you can lay the foundation for a productive dialogue.

HONESTY AND TRANSPARENCY

Being direct can often be difficult in any relationship. But you can be direct without hurting her feelings by following some of the key communication components here. The conversation about your desire to obtain a prenuptial agreement should be had as soon as you know you want one, and the further away from the wedding, the better. You will need to be honest with yourself and your partner about your aspirations, dreams, and concerns.

Creating a safe space for open communication without fear of judgment is crucial. If you do not feel that you have this opportunity in your relationship, it might be easier to have this conversation in front of a relationship therapist, counselor, or pastor. However you create a safe space for these important conversations, you will need to be upfront about why you believe a prenuptial agreement is necessary and what specific concerns you have about your financial future.

I am not suggesting that you enter into this conversation with your significant other as if you were in some high-stakes negotiation that you might have seen on an attorney-themed television show. Instead, I recommend that you lay all your metaphorical cards out and be completely honest about what you want out of life with your significant other.

ACTIVE LISTENING

You may want to employ active listening in all parts of your circles. Lawyers are keen to listen to clues about what people want to know, what to ask for and know when to settle, and how to settle a case. This is called compromise, which is literally defined as "a settlement of differences by mutual concessions; an agreement reached by adjustment of conflicting or opposing claims, principles, etc., by reciprocal modification of demands."

Practice active listening techniques are crucial, such as maintaining eye contact, looking for non-verbal cues, asking open-ended questions, and paraphrasing to demonstrate understanding and build trust. It might sound like parroting to you, but it is important to repeat your understanding of what is being requested so that you are clear on your goal, and your fiancé's goals, so that by the end of the conversation you have an agreement.

According to the American Bar Association, in an article called "How to Improve Lawyer and Client Communications" by Jenna Burnell published in November 2023, active listening involves maintaining good eye contact (even on a video call!), looking for non-verbal cues like physical signs of anxiety, sadness, or anger, and using those cues to offer appropriate support, asking open-ended questions to gain more information and express genuine interest, and paraphrasing the speaker's words and reflecting them back to demonstrate close attention. The goal is to make the speaker feel heard and understood and to create trust in the relationship.

MUTUAL RESPECT AND EMPATHY

Approach the conversation with mutual respect and empathy, understanding that disagreement does not necessarily equate to a lack of understanding. Focus on finding common ground and shared goals. Recognize that your partner may have valid concerns or fears about prenuptial agreements and be prepared to address these openly and respectfully.

You can agree to disagree and still move forward on certain issues. Understanding doesn't necessarily equate to agreement, but it does lay the foundation for productive dialogue. The key is to determine if the issue is a barrier to reaching a shared goal. You need to determine if the disagreement will create a "deal breaker." Sometimes people get so caught up in disagreement that they fail to see that there is room for agreement elsewhere.

FOCUS ON SOLUTIONS

Instead of dwelling on disagreements, focus on finding solutions and common ground that align with both partners' goals and values. This may involve brainstorming different approaches to financial planning and protection that can satisfy both parties.

SETTING GROUND RULES FOR CONSTRUCTIVE COMMUNICATION

Establishing ground rules can provide a structured framework for constructive communication and help navigate potentially sensitive topics. By agreeing on guidelines for the discussion, you can create a safe and supportive environment where both partners feel heard and understood.

Lawyers use their pleadings and notes to frame thoughts and arguments that they want to address with the court. While you will not be in this environment when you have this conversation, if there is a chance that the conversation could broach a sensitive topic, approaching it with some guidelines could help keep tempers in check and the conversation on track. Therefore, if you think you need notes or an agenda, there's nothing wrong with it, if your significant other agrees that the topics of discussion are what are listed on that document.

OPEN-MINDEDNESS

This topic goes back to establishing a safe space that is free from judgment. In conversations with your significant other about your desire for a prenup, you should approach the discussion with an open mind. This means that you should be willing to consider different perspectives and ideas. Understand that your partner may have different viewpoints and be willing to listen and incorporate their feedback into the discussion.

PRACTICAL TIPS FOR BREAKING THE NEWS

When approaching the subject of a prenuptial agreement, timing, setting, and the manner in which you bring up the topic are all crucial. Here are some practical tips to help you navigate this sensitive conversation:

Choose the Right Time and Place

Find a quiet, private setting where you can talk without interruptions. Avoid bringing up the topic during stressful times or when either of you is likely to be distracted or preoccupied.

Be Clear About Your Intentions

Start the conversation by expressing your love and commitment to your partner. Explain that the prenuptial agreement is not about mistrust but about planning for the future and protecting both parties' interests.

Use "I" Statements

Frame your reasons for wanting a prenup in terms of your own feelings and concerns. For example, say, "I feel that a prenuptial agreement could help us avoid potential conflicts in the future" rather than, "You need to sign a prenup."

Discuss the Benefits

Highlight the potential benefits of a prenuptial agreement, such as financial clarity, protection of individual assets, and the prevention of future disputes. Emphasize that the agreement can provide security and peace of mind for both parties.

Address Concerns and Questions

Be prepared to listen to your partner's concerns and answer any questions they may have. This is where active listening and empathy are especially important. Acknowledge their feelings and reassure them that you are open to discussing any modifications to the agreement.

THE IMPORTANCE OF PROFESSIONAL GUIDANCE

Seeking guidance from professionals can help facilitate the conversation and ensure that both parties fully understand the implications of a prenuptial agreement. Involving a family law attorney and possibly a financial advisor can provide valuable insights and support. Attorneys and financial advisors have the expertise to explain the legal and financial aspects of prenuptial agreements. They can help clarify complex issues and provide objective advice.

A neutral third party can help mediate the discussion and ensure that both partners' interests are fairly represented. This can be especially helpful if emotions run high or if there are significant disagreements. You do not need to go out and hire a mediator. Again, this conversation can occur with a relationship counselor or therapist.

REAL LIFE EXAMPLE: THE SETUP (WHAT NOT TO DO)

A young woman came to see me for representation on a prenuptial agreement. She did not know she was coming to my office to discuss a prenuptial agreement because she only spoke Spanish and her soon-to-be-husband did not. Apparently, her fiancé had booked the appointment. So, on the day of her appointment, when I met with her, she handed me a prenuptial agreement, and I started reading it to myself. I then asked her in Spanish if she read it. She clearly had not because she did not read English.

I started reviewing the agreement with her page by page so that she understood what the agreement said, and

I wanted to know what she thought about it. As I read it, she looked stunned. She told me she had no idea that the agreement said what it said. She had never discussed the terms with her fiancé. (Her fiancé let me be the one to break the news to her about what he wanted.) She started crying. I felt so bad for her.

Without getting into the specifics of the agreement, your lawyer should not be the person who is breaking the news to your fiancé about the terms of a prenup or that you even want one to begin with. This will set the tone for the rest of the relationship, and for this reason, it is important to practice the above communication skills to start your marriage off on the right foot.

CONCLUSION

Breaking the news that you want a prenuptial agreement requires careful consideration and effective communication skills. By approaching the conversation with honesty, empathy, and respect, you can create a safe space for open dialogue and foster understanding between partners. Remember to practice active listening, set ground rules for constructive communication, and focus on finding common ground and shared goals. With these strategies, you can navigate the discussion with confidence and lay the foundation for a strong and resilient relationship.

16

ROADBLOCKS TO A PRENUP

While navigating the process of obtaining a prenuptial agreement, you can encounter various roadblocks, ranging from practical challenges to emotional hurdles. In this chapter, we will explore the obstacles you may face in initiating and completing the prenup process, including considerations of time, cost, family dynamics, and emotional implications. By understanding these potential roadblocks, you can give yourself ample time to navigate them effectively and obtain a prenup before marriage.

COST CONSIDERATIONS

Prenuptial agreements can be costly, both in terms of financial expenses and emotional investment. Attorney fees for hiring lawyers to draft and review the agreement can add up quickly depending on how much time your attorney spends with you drafting and negotiating any edits to the agreement. Moreover, each party must have their own legal representation to ensure that their interests are adequately protected and that they fully understand the rights they are waiving. You may find yourself paying for the fees of her attorney, too. Remember, just because you pay for her attorney fees does not entitle you to any attorney-client privileged communications. So, you will not have the right to any firsthand communication from her lawyer. All communications regarding edits to the agreement will come from the lawyer. This does not mean that you cannot communicate changes to the agreement with your fiancé. It just means that her lawyer is not allowed to speak to you.

Legal fees for drafting a prenuptial agreement can range from a few thousand dollars to tens of thousands, depending on the complexity of the assets and the negotiations involved. Additionally, if the agreement is challenged in court later, the costs can escalate further, potentially involving extensive legal battles and the need for expert witnesses, such as forensic accountants or financial analysts. It may be cheaper to amend the agreement later with mutually satisfactory terms that are enforceable than to leave it to the lawyers to fight about in a divorce.

There is also an emotional cost to consider. Discussions about finances and the potential end of a marriage can be stressful and emotionally draining. For logical reasons, you should have these conversations early on in your relationship. It is important to be prepared for these conversations as it gets closer to the signing of the prenuptial agreement and to approach them with sensitivity and care.

TIME CONSTRAINTS

Initiating and finalizing a prenuptial agreement requires time and careful consideration. Rushing the process can lead to oversights or mistakes, while procrastination can leave you without the necessary protections in place before marriage. Ideally, the process should begin several months before the wedding to allow ample time for discussions, negotiations, and revisions.

The timeline for drafting a prenup typically includes initial discussions, gathering financial documents, consulting with attorneys, drafting the agreement, and reviewing and revising the document. Each step can take time, especially if there are complex assets or significant differences in financial status between the partners.

It's also important to consider that both parties need to have a clear mind and be free from external pressures when negotiating the prenup. Engaging in this process too close to the wedding date can add unnecessary stress and may even result in the agreement being contested later on the grounds of duress or coercion.

ENFORCEABILITY CONCERNS

Not all prenuptial agreements are enforceable, particularly if they are deemed unconscionable or unfair at the time of enforcement. Understanding the legal requirements and potential challenges associated with prenups is essential for ensuring their validity and effectiveness.

An agreement may be considered unenforceable if it is found to be excessively one-sided, was signed under duress, or did not include full financial disclosure from both parties. For example, a prenup that leaves one spouse destitute while the other retains all the assets may be seen as unconscionable. Similarly, if one party was pressured into signing the agreement shortly before the wedding, they might later argue that they were under duress.

California law, for instance, requires that both parties have at least seven days to review the agreement before signing it, and that both parties have access to independent legal counsel. Failing to meet these requirements can render the agreement invalid.

FUTURE CONSIDERATIONS

Circumstances and priorities may change over time, rendering certain provisions of the prenup obsolete or impractical. It's important to consider the long-term implications of the agreement and be prepared to revisit and potentially update it as needed.

For instance, a provision that makes sense at the time of marriage may not be relevant twenty years down the line. Changes in financial status, career advancements, the birth of children, or even health issues can all impact the fairness and applicability of a prenuptial agreement.

Regularly reviewing and updating the prenup can help address these changes. You could consider a sunset clause that specifies a period after which the prenup expires or by adding provisions that require periodic reviews and updates.

FAMILY DYNAMICS

Family members may have strong opinions or objections regarding the decision to pursue a prenup, adding additional layers of complexity to the process. Balancing familial expectations with your own needs and priorities can be challenging but necessary for ensuring that the agreement reflects your best interests.

Parents are usually the main driving force behind the requirement of a prenup. Sometimes, I am caught between a parent, who is paying the legal fees to my office, and the client, who is trying to get married. The parent wants to make sure that everything is being handled but the client is not communicating with the parent in the way in which the parent is expecting. So, I will get a phone call from the client's mother, for example. As I discussed in earlier chapters, parents have their own ideas about how to maintain generational wealth that they, or their parents or other family members, may have created.

On the other hand, some parents may have concerns about the implications of a prenuptial agreement. They might worry that it suggests a lack of trust in the relationship or that it could create tension between the partners.

It's important to communicate openly with family members about a prenuptial agreement. You may need to reassure them that it is a practical step to protect both parties' interests. Emphasize that the prenup is not about mistrust but about planning for the future and ensuring financial security for both partners.

PERSONAL FEELINGS

Discussing a prenup can evoke a range of emotions, including anxiety, fear, and discomfort. It's important to approach these discussions with empathy and understanding, recognizing that both of you may have valid concerns and perspectives.

The idea of planning for a potential divorce can be unsettling and may lead to feelings of insecurity or doubt about the relationship. One partner might feel that the request for a prenup indicates a lack of confidence in the marriage, while the other might worry about protecting their financial assets.

To navigate these emotional challenges, it's crucial to create a safe and supportive environment for discussions. Practice active listening, validate each other's feelings, and focus on the benefits of having a clear and mutually agreed-upon plan for the future.

STRATEGIES FOR OVERCOMING ROADBLOCKS

Allocate Sufficient Time and Resources

To navigate the practical challenges of obtaining a prenup, allocate sufficient time and resources to the process. Start discussions early, engage qualified legal professionals, and be prepared for the financial costs involved.

Seek Legal Guidance

Engaging an experienced family law attorney is crucial for drafting a prenuptial agreement that is legally sound and enforceable. Both parties should have their own legal representation to ensure that their interests are adequately protected and that they fully understand the terms of the agreement.

Approach Discussions with Empathy

Approach discussions about the prenuptial agreement with empathy and understanding. Recognize that both partners may have valid concerns and emotions about the process. Create a safe space for open and honest communication and be prepared to listen and address each other's fears and doubts.

Balance Family Expectations

Balancing family expectations with personal needs can be challenging, but it's important to communicate openly with family members about the reasons for wanting a prenup. Reassure them that the agreement is a practical step to protect both parties' interests and ensure financial security for the future.

EXAMPLES: NAVIGATING ROADBLOCKS

Example 1: Financial Costs and Time Management

Jane and Michael decided to get a prenuptial agreement, but they underestimated the financial costs and the time required to finalize it. They sought legal advice early and were transparent about their financial situations. Fortunately, they allocated a portion of their wedding budget to cover legal fees and set a timeline that allowed for thorough discussions and revisions. By planning ahead and managing their time effectively, Jane and Michael were able to finalize a fair and comprehensive prenuptial agreement without compromising their wedding plans.

Example 2: Emotional and Family Dynamics

Wendy wanted a prenuptial agreement to protect her family business, but her fiancé, Harry, felt hurt and offended by the request. Wendy's parents also had strong opinions in support of the prenup, adding to the tension. Wendy and Harry engaged in open and honest discussions about their concerns and sought the help of a mediator to facilitate the conversation. Wendy explained her reasons for wanting the prenup and reassured Harry of her commitment to their relationship. Through empathy and active listening, Wendy and Harry were able to reach an agreement that protected both their interests. The couple moved forward with their wedding plans.

CONCLUSION

Navigating the roadblocks to obtaining a prenuptial agreement requires careful consideration of practical, legal, and emotional factors. By acknowledging the challenges and proactively addressing them, you can increase the likelihood of successfully completing the prenup process and securing your financial future. Remember to allocate sufficient time and resources, seek legal guidance, and approach discussions with empathy and understanding. With patience, diligence, and open communication, you can overcome the roadblocks and achieve a prenup that provides peace of mind and financial security for you and your partner.

THERE GO THE WEDDING BELLS

As we approach the culmination of our journey through the intricacies of prenuptial agreements, it's essential to reflect on the valuable lessons and insights gained along the way. In this chapter, we will recapitulate the key points discussed in previous chapters and reinforce the importance of proactive planning and decision-making when it comes to prenups.

RECAPITULATION OF KEY LEARNINGS

Throughout this book, we have explored a multitude of topics related to prenuptial agreements, each shedding light on different aspects of their significance and implications for individuals entering into marriage.

Here's a brief overview of the key learnings from each chapter.

Chapter 1: I Work Hard for My Money

Chapter 1 focused on understanding the need for a

prenup to protect your assets, income, and financial future. We discussed how a prenup can help delineate what belongs to each spouse and prevent contentious disputes over property division in the event of a divorce.

Chapter 2: Finding the Right Lawyer

In this chapter, you learned about choosing the best legal representation to guide you through the prenup process effectively. We emphasized the importance of selecting a lawyer who specializes in family law and has experience with prenuptial agreements.

Chapter 3: What You Need to Know

This chapter highlighted how to initiate conversations with your partner about prenups and understanding the importance of clear communication in the process. This chapter provided a roadmap of the topics covered in the book and highlighted the significance of transparency and mutual respect in these discussions.

Chapter 4: A Prenup Is Not Something One Does on a Whim

Chapter 4 discussed recognizing the legal steps and considerations involved in drafting and finalizing a prenuptial agreement. We explored the detailed process, from initial discussions to the signing of the document, stressing the importance of careful planning and due diligence.

Chapter 5: The Terms of the Prenup

Here you learned to understand the various provisions and protections that can be included in a prenup to address specific concerns and goals. We covered topics such as asset protection, debt responsibility, income, investments, retirement plans, inheritance, and spousal support.

Chapter 6: What Happens When You Do Not Get a Prenup in California

This chapter was about grasping the potential consequences of not having a prenup, particularly in community property states like California. This chapter highlighted how assets and debts acquired during the marriage would be divided equally upon divorce, regardless of individual contributions.

Chapter 7: Protecting the Money Given to You

In this chapter, we addressed inheritance protection issues and the importance of safeguarding separate property assets. We discussed how to keep inherited money or gifts from family separate from marital property.

Chapter 8: The House You Bought Before Marriage

Chapter 8 focused on understanding how separate property assets can acquire community property interests and the need for provisions to protect them in a prenup.

We examined the complexities of property ownership and mortgage payments made during the marriage.

Chapter 9: Reimbursements for Stuff Paid for before Marriage

Moving on, we explored the legal complexities surrounding reimbursements for premarital expenses and liabilities. This chapter explained how to handle reimbursements for significant expenditures made before marriage that benefited both partners.

Chapter 10: Protecting Your Income and Retirement

Chapter 10 addressed the potential impact of marriage on income, retirement assets, and business interests, and the need for prenup provisions to protect them. We delved into protecting bonuses, employer-sponsored retirement contributions, stock options, and business interests.

Chapter 11: A Gift May Not Always Be a Gift

Understanding the distinction between gifts before and during marriage and their implications for property division in divorce was the focus of Chapter 11. We discussed how to clearly define gifts in a prenup to avoid disputes.

Chapter 12: Staying Out of Your Fiancé's Potential Legal Issues

Next, we recognized the importance of protecting each other from potential legal liabilities and debts. We highlighted strategies to shield one another from business risks and personal debts.

Chapter 13: Children and Child Support

When getting a prenup, understanding the limitations of including terms related to future children and child support in a prenup is also important. This chapter emphasized that child support provisions must comply with state laws and cannot be predetermined in a prenup.

Chapter 14: Spousal Support

This chapter covered exploring strategies for addressing spousal support provisions in a prenup effectively. We discussed how to create fair and reasonable spousal support clauses that consider income disparity and the duration of the marriage.

Chapter 15: How to Break the News That You Want a Prenup

In this chapter, you learned lawyer tips for initiating discussions about prenups with your partner and fostering open communication. This chapter provided practical advice on how to approach this sensitive topic with empathy and understanding.

Chapter 16: Roadblocks to a Prenup

Finally, we identified potential obstacles and challenges in obtaining a prenuptial agreement and strategies for overcoming them. We explored issues such as time constraints, cost considerations, family dynamics, and emotional implications.

FINAL THOUGHTS AND ANECDOTES

As we conclude our journey, it's important to reiterate the significance of proactive planning and decision-making when it comes to prenuptial agreements. Remember, a prenup isn't just about protecting assets; it's about establishing clear expectations, promoting open communication, and safeguarding the future of your relationship.

Throughout my years as a family law attorney, I have witnessed firsthand the transformative impact of prenuptial agreements on couples' lives. From protecting hard-earned assets to preserving peace of mind and marital harmony, the benefits of a well-crafted prenup are undeniable.

The Importance of Timing

It's crucial not to wait until the last minute to consider a prenup. Procrastination can lead to rushed decisions, oversights, and missed opportunities for meaningful dialogue with your partner. By giving yourself ample time to explore the possibilities and discuss your concerns openly and honestly, you can lay the foundation for a strong and resilient marriage built on trust, understanding, and mutual respect.

Engaging in these discussions well before the wedding date allows both of you to approach the topic with a clear mind and without external pressures. This ensures that the agreement is entered into voluntarily and thoughtfully, reducing the risk of future disputes.

Practical Steps for Finalizing Your Prenup

- **Start Early**: Begin the process of obtaining a prenup several months before your wedding to allow ample time for discussions, negotiations, and revisions.
- **Seek Legal Advice**: Engage experienced family law attorneys to guide you through the process and ensure that the agreement complies with state laws.
- **Full Financial Disclosure**: Both parties should provide complete and honest disclosure of their financial situations, including assets, liabilities, income, and any other relevant financial information.
- **Drafting the Agreement**: Work with your attorneys to draft the prenuptial agreement, ensuring that it addresses all relevant issues and reflects your mutual interests and values.
- **Review and Revise**: Carefully review the draft agreement and discuss any necessary revisions with your partner and your attorney.
- **Sign and Notarize**: Once the agreement is finalized, both parties should sign it in the presence of a notary to ensure that it is legally binding and enforceable.

- **Regular Updates**: Consider revisiting and updating the prenuptial agreement periodically, like when you reach major life milestones or after many years of marriage to reflect any changes in your financial situation or personal circumstances.

CONCLUSION

As we conclude our exploration of prenuptial agreements, you'll be equipped with a comprehensive overview of the prenup journey. By embracing open communication, commencing in a timely manner, and understanding that negotiation is an important process that will create mutual understanding of the life goals that each of you has, you will be well-prepared to navigate the legal process to obtain a mutually satisfactory prenuptial agreement with confidence and clarity, laying the groundwork for a secure and prosperous marital journey.

In closing, I hope this book has provided you with valuable insights, guidance, and reassurance as you navigate the complexities of prenuptial agreements. Remember, you don't have to face this journey alone. Seek the support and guidance of experienced legal professionals to help you make informed decisions and embark on this new chapter of your life with confidence and peace of mind.

As you hear the wedding bells ring, may they signify not just the beginning of a new chapter, but also the promise of a future filled with love, partnership, and shared prosperity. By being proactive and well-informed, you can create a strong and supportive foundation for your future together.

A FINAL WORD OF ENCOURAGEMENT

Embarking on the journey of drafting a prenuptial agreement can be daunting, but it is a step that demonstrates foresight and commitment to the well-being of both partners. It is a practical measure that ensures financial clarity and reduces the potential for conflict in the future.

Remember, a prenuptial agreement is not just a legal document; it is a testament to the strength of your relationship and your mutual respect for each other's financial independence and security. By approaching the process with an open heart and mind, you can create an agreement that honors your partnership and sets the stage for a harmonious and fulfilling marriage.

Congratulations on taking this important step towards securing your future together. May your marriage be filled with joy, love, and lasting happiness.

ACKNOWLEDGMENTS

I want to thank my mom, Tina, for always being there for me and my little family. Without her I could not do half of the things I want to do. My kids, Ruby and Conan, are well attended to in her care, and I get fed at least once a day.

I want to also thank the staff and attorneys at Genesis Family Law for putting up with my wild ideas. I don't think anyone knew what I meant when I said I was writing a book, or that I perhaps could actually finish it. But here it is, and I thank you all for supporting me by handling the things I couldn't while concentrating on this project.

I want to thank my friends – you know who you are – who just give me so much emotional support and encouragement. It surprises me when you are not surprised that I am doing half of the things I do as if you expect me to keep saying wild things.

Finally, I want to thank my clients for being a source of inspiration.

Thank you!!!!

ABOUT THE AUTHOR

Leslie Abrigo is a family law attorney with more than twenty years of experience helping couples to begin their married lives off on the strongest foundation.

In 2024, she was recognized as a top lawyer in California by the *Daily Journal*. In 2024, she was also recognized as a Top 25 San Diego Woman Lawyer by Super Lawyers. In 2021, she was awarded the Mike C. Shea Award from the San Diego Family Law Bar Association. In 2018, she was recognized as Lawyer of the Year by the San Diego South Bay Bar Association.

Ms. Abrigo has made numerous legal education presentations including How to Prepare an Ironclad DOD for the National Conflict Resolution Center and Continuing Education of the Bar (CEB). She has also presented on family law and immigration cross-over issues and set-asides of agreements in family court. She has lectured on discovery as a guest lecturer for the Family Law Class at California Western School of Law on several occasions.

She has recently published *The Prenup Workbook: A Different Kind of Marriage Planning* and *The Postnup*

Workbook: A Different Way to Address Financial Marital Concerns. Both are available on Amazon.

She is a graduate of the California Western School of Law and obtained her undergraduate degree from the University of Puget Sound. She is fluent in Spanish and English. In her spare time, in addition to writing, she enjoys spending time with her children, Ruby and Conan.

- Website: https://genesisfamilylaw.com/attorney/leslie-l-abrigo/
- Email: abrigo@genesisfamilylaw.com
- Instagram: @chulavistafamilylaw
- Facebook: @Leslie L Abrigo, APC
- TikTok: @greatfamilylawyer

ABOUT DIFFERENCE PRESS

Difference Press is the publishing arm of The Author Incubator, an Inc. 500 award-winning company that helps business owners and executives grow their brand, establish thought leadership, and get customers, clients, and highly-paid speaking opportunities, through writing and publishing books.

While traditional publishers require that you already have a large following to guarantee they make money from sales to your existing list, our approach is focused on using a book to grow your following – even if you currently don't have a following. This is why we charge an up-front fee but never take a percentage of revenue you earn from your book.

☞ MORE THAN A COACH. MORE THAN A PUBLISHER. ✍

We work intimately and personally with each of our authors to develop a revenue-generating strategy for the book. By using a Lean Startup style methodology, we guarantee the book's success before we even start writing. We provide all the technical support authors need with editing, design, marketing, and publishing, the emotional support you would get from a book coach to help you manage anxiety and time constraints, and we serve as a strategic thought partner engineering the book for success.

The Author Incubator has helped almost 2,000 entrepreneurs write, publish, and promote their non-fiction books. Our authors have used their books to gain international media exposure, build a brand and marketing following, get lucrative speaking engagements, raise awareness of their product or service, and attract clients and customers.

☞ ARE YOU READY TO WRITE A BOOK? ✍

As a client, we will work with you to make sure your book gets done right and that it gets done quickly. The Author Incubator provides one-stop for strategic book consultation, author coaching to manage writer's block and anxiety, full-service professional editing, design, and self-publishing services, and book marketing and launch campaigns. We sell this as one package so our clients are not slowed down with contradictory advice. We have a 99 percent success rate with nearly all of our clients completing their books, publishing them, and reaching bestseller status upon launch.

☞ APPLY NOW AND BE OUR NEXT SUCCESS STORY ✍

To find out if there is a significant ROI for you to write a book, get on our calendar by completing an application at www.TheAuthorIncubator.com/apply.

OTHER BOOKS BY DIFFERENCE PRESS

Fragile: Handle with Care: Living and Loving with an Ehlers-Danlos Syndrome (EDS) Diagnosis by Julee Cruz

The Family Business Guru: A Secret Guide to Alchemize Conflict into Harmony, Lead with Confidence, and Generate Profits by Avadhi Dhruv

Fundraising without Burnout: Radically Reimagining Philanthropy to Transform Your Impact by Radha Friedman

Always Bring Your Sunglasses: And Other Stories from a Life of Sensory and Social Invalidation by Becca Lory Hector

The Inclusion Illusion: An HR Guide to Educating Executives on DEI by Katherine Longhi

Living Intentionally after Loss: 8 Steps to Reclaiming Your Passion and Purpose by Maya Manseau

Breakthrough to Entrepreneurial Brilliance: Shatter the Invisible Barrier Holding Your Business Back by Alana Mills

The Empathetic Attorney: Advocating for Survivors of Sexual Violence through Trauma Informed Care by AnnaMarie Motis

Is This a Cult?: Confronting the Line between Transformation and Exploitation by Anne. L. Peterson

Founder to Exit: A CFO's Blueprint for Small Business Owners by Pam Prior

A Second Wind after Loss: A Guide to Health and Renewed Purpose for the Grieving Heart by Denise Sherman

GIFT FOR READER

Thank you so much for reading, *Before "I Do:" The Lawyer's Guide to Proposing a Prenup*. If you have reached the end of the book, it tells me that you are committed to being upfront and transparent with your fiancé. It also tells me that at least in terms of communicating, you are on the right path to working out any marital disputes.

I would like to learn more about your path to prenuptial planning. Please keep in touch by visiting my website at www.genesisfamilylaw.com.

If you are looking for further support, and want to get your hands on a copy of either one of my workbooks, you can find them at the links below:

- *The Prenup Workbook: A Different Kind of Marriage Planning*
- *The Postnup Workbook: A Different Way to Address Financial Marital Concerns*

You can also find me on all social media platforms, but I am most active on TikTok @greatfamilylawyer. Tag me in your posts with #Prenupbook. I would love to see how you are doing.

www.ingramcontent.com/pod-product-compliance
Lightning Source LLC
Chambersburg PA
CBHW052201220526
45471CB00004B/1759